LET SOUTH AFRICA SHINE

Reflections, Insights and Solutions as seen through the eyes of a humble Voter

Citizen S.A.

CONTENTS

WHO AM I?

INEVER HAD ANY INTEREST IN POLITICS. When I was young, my father would frequently remark that politics is a dirty game. His advice was to stay away from politics and live a simple and honest life. And that was all he would say leaving the rest up to my imagination to make sense of his inexplicable outbursts that branded all politicians as bad and immoral. Although my young mind did not really understand what this all meant, I made up my mind not to venture into politics and I shunned everything that showed a hint of being political. I made a concerted effort to live an uneventful yet honest and law-abiding existence.

Yet here I am writing this book that has forced me into this murky underworld of politics. A world comprising of arrogant, self-centred, dishonest, deceitful, greedy and corrupt politicians. A world with only a sprinkling of honest politicians with integrity smothered by their corrupt counterparts. There is an obvious lack of accountability in politics and citizens appear on the surface to accept this. Within this bizarre scenario, I dare ask myself the obvious questions, "Would it not be easier and beneficial to all if the rules of politics were changed to attract honest and ordinary people into politics?" and "How would a political landscape where Politicians choose to operate with integrity putting the interest of their citizens first look like?"

I was born in the sixties in a town in South Africa. I had my fair share of apartheid, trying to come to terms with the notion of being a lower-class citizen in the country of my birth. My future was determined by the colour of my skin, but I was determined not to let this hold me back. Whatever the future held for me, I was determined to succeed. Despite my almost hopeless situation, I lived an honest, moral life far removed from politics. I went to a primary school that initially had those horrible bucket toilets and I still remember how relieved I was when they were converted to proper sewerage toilets. It pains me to think that in our twenty first century and democratic country, our people and children are still using bucket and pit toilets. The reported child deaths in pit toilets due to the lack of maintenance is heart wrenching especially with the realisation that the money set aside to upgrade this infrastructure is lining the pockets of our politicians and their allies. I now truly understand what my father was alluding to when he said that politics is a dirty game.

My childhood was consumed with thinking of ways to realise my dreams and have a great life despite the apartheid regime weighing heavily on my future goals. I was however lucky enough to be in my early twenties when Nelson Mandela was released, and South Africa became a democracy. The opportunities were endless and realising my dreams became easier and more realistic. Most of all, this new beautiful and democratic country with exciting opportunities needed young people like me to be part of this change. I decided to remain in South Africa despite the opportunities abroad that was available to young people like myself. At that time this proved to be the best decision and I enjoyed the freedom and the positivity that my country had to offer. Nelson Mandela was at the helm steering Brand South Africa away from a shrouded insignificant African country to an admired and celebrated country that attracted worldwide affirmations and investments.

Thabo Mbeki took the baton from Mandela and largely continued the good work of making South Africa a global player. I guess many South Africans like myself were so caught up in the positivity and growth opportunities in our country that we never saw Jacob Zuma coming. When Zuma was elected as president in 2009, I was indifferent despite the numerous legal scandals of corruption and racketeering that shadowed him. I guess I still had the euphoric Mandela spirit and assumed that Zuma will take the baton from Mbeki and surround himself with good people who will continue the great work of our previous leaders. I was wrong. Yes, I was so wrong! Zuma was supposed to be just a figurehead. Zuma epitomised the political face that my father described so many years ago. The face of politics being a dirty game filled with corruption, scandals, theft in the form of state capture that benefits a select few scalawags at the expense of honest citizens who just want to live a peaceful law-abiding life.

My one regret is that although my children were born in our democratic South Africa, they were too small to experience the Mandela and Mbeki era. Their experience of living in South Africa is the Zuma years and they hate it so much and sadly see no future for themselves in their birth country. I am constantly being asked why I did not leave South Africa when I was younger so that they could have a better future. They cannot comprehend my decision to be part of a so-called Democratic country that has not delivered to the youth and South Africa as a whole.

However, despite the current failings, I strongly believe that South Africa can thrive once again and be the great country it set out to be post-apartheid. I believe that this journey will not be as onerous if we collectively put our minds together and work as a nation to rebuild our country. This belief has motivated me to share my thoughts and create my road map for this journey in the hope that there are more people like myself feeling the aftermath of the Zuma regime, observing the current mudslinging between and among political parties, waking up every day frustrated and wondering what the day will reveal about state capture or other shenanigans in our political arena.

I write this book in the hope that these people will also be inspired to move South Africa towards its rightful democratic path and find a platform to share their road maps too. This would lead to a collective solution created by ordinary South Africans providing solutions to set our country on the right trajectory. In my opinion vocalising our thoughts are better than keeping them in our mind while our politicians chart the way forward for us. Most importantly, let's do this for our children, let's get out of our comfort zone, let's get cracking.

CHAPTER 1: CAN THE RULING PARTY PUT SOUTH AFRICA BACK ON TRACK?

L ET'S FACE IT – THE ANC (AFRICAN NATIONAL CONGRESS) was instrumental in transforming South Africa from racial oppression to democratic political freedom. The ANC under Mandela and Mbeki were all embracing, inclusive and strived for non-racial unity. They worked towards creating a country that belonged to all who live in it. In Fact, Mandela in his 1994 presidential inauguration speech said:

"The moment to bridge the chasms that divide us has come."

"We enter into a covenant that we shall build the society in which all South Africans, both black and white, will be able to walk tall, without any fear in their hearts, assured of their inalienable right to human dignity - a rainbow nation at peace with itself and the world."

"We must therefore act together as a united people, for national reconciliation, for nation building, for the birth of a new world"

Mandela with his Government of National Unity and Mbeki were dedicated to transformation of South Africa striving for national unity. Attaining national unity was the key to neutralising the malicious tendencies and remnants of apartheid. This was the era that heralded political freedom for all – a post-apartheid, democratic South Africa epitomised by an independent media and judiciary with strong opposition parties keeping the ruling party in check. Sadly, political democracy is meaningless if it does not improve the physical circumstances of the people.

While the ANC brought political democracy to South Africa, it failed, especially in the Zuma era, to deliver its vision of economic democracy to the people. The impoverished reality experienced by most South Africans today is understated by our Politicians and Government who seem oblivious of the blatant daily humiliation that undermines the people's right to dignity. This flies in the face of Nelson Mandela's ANC Government of National Unity and promise of poverty alleviation. Since 2007 South Africa has spiraled into a political and economic quagmire with no inkling on how to get back on the path of good governance, economic freedom and national unity. The ANC is suffering from a bipolar party disorder – At face value, it represents the heroic party that led South Africa to freedom but probing the underbelly of the ANC reveals sordid corruption, state capture and thuggery.

What we need is good honest political leadership and a strong leader who is willing to put the needs of the people above the political party he or she serves. We need a leader who is passionate about improving the lives of all South Africans as opposed to lining the pockets of other politicians willing to drive his or her personal agenda. We need a leader who is willing to take tough moral and political decisions for the advancement of our country. We need a leader with the heart of Mandela, the strong will of Mbeki, the conscience of Archbishop Desmond Tutu and the business acumen of Cyril Ramaphosa.

Does the ANC have the right leader?

Cyril Ramaphosa is a smart business leader. He has the Mandela spirit and is a man with a conscience. Ramaphosa needs Mbeki's strong will to complete the package especially when it comes to getting rid of blatant incompetence, corruption and the dead wood in his Party and Government. I was thrilled when Ramaphosa was elected as ANC president in December 2016 and subsequently President of South Africa in February 2018. The dark era of the Zuma rule had eventually ended, and democratic South Africa was given a second chance. We had the right leader in place to succeed in moving our country forward (or so I thought). I had that same optimistic feeling I had when Mandela was elected president.

Sadly, this optimism was short lived when Ramaphosa announced his new cabinet and I was horrified to see the likes of Bathabile Dlamini and Nomvula Mokonyane still in the cabinet. Malusi Gigaba who is alleged to have been linked to state capture was also rewarded by Ramaphosa with the Home Affairs Ministry (his previous portfolio that gave the Guptas citizenship). He eventually resigned after much controversy but could be back in Cabinet after the May elections. Ironically the ANC praised Gigaba for putting the country first.

Is this the calibre of leaders that the ANC support? The Water and Sanitation Ministry under Mokonyane's watch was bankrupt and on the brink of collapse when she was rewarded with yet another critical ministry, namely Communications and has recently become the Minister of Environmental Affairs. She has also been fingered out as having an alleged corrupt relationship with the Bosasa Facilities Management Company which she has not publicly refuted. She is still in Cyril's Cabinet and probably will be after the May elections. Bathabile Dlamini who repeatedly gambled with the livelihood of the most vulnerable (SASSA - South African Social Security Agency debacle) was rewarded with the portfolio of Women Ministry in the Presidency. These vulnerable people that receive grants are the elderly, children and disabled. These appointments undoubtedly indicated the tendency for Ramaphosa to try to please all – his Party and the People.

When Mbeki fired Zuma in 2005 because of his "corrupt relationship" with Schabir Shaik, he took parliament and the nation into his confidence by doing what was best for the country. This decisiveness and strong conviction are what Ramaphosa is shying away from. In 1995, President Mandela fired his wife Winnie Madikizela-Mandela, as Deputy Arts and Culture Minister for her alleged attacks on government policy and embarrassing scandals. These are trivial in comparison to the self-serving mischiefs of Bathabile Dlamini. Yet Bathabile Dlamini who in my opinion should have been fired when Ramaphosa announced his first Cabinet is still around. President Ramaphosa may have forgotten that he has the prerogative to dismiss members of his cabinet and is accountable first to the people of South Africa and then his Party.

Ramaphosa's indecisiveness can also be exemplified in the events of the Life Esidimeni tragedy. This tragedy resulted in 144 mental health patients losing their lives and more than 1000 patients living in torturous circumstances. Justice Dikgang Moseneke in his Life Esidimeni arbitration report singled out the former health MEC (Member of the Executive Council) Qedani Mahlangu as being the architect behind this tragedy and recommended that criminal investigations be undertaken, and the charge of culpable homicide be explored. Instead of criminal and legal actions being taken against her, Mahlangu was rewarded by being elected into the ANC's Provincial Executive Committee (PEC). Only recently (10 December 2018) was she removed from this position, but her ANC membership has not been revoked. This implies that the ANC has no problem with unethical people like her representing it. The unwillingness to take decisive action against people responsible for heinous acts against our people is disheartening. The State Capture and other enquiries have been commissioned. The appointment of Shamila Batohi as Head of the National Prosecuting Authority is a positive move in the fight against corruption. There is still no criminal prosecution but let's hope that this will follow soon.

What South Africans need is for the people responsible for the current dire economic crisis to face the law of our country.   We also need a ruling Party that carries the will of the people in their heart. My advice to Ramaphosa is that sometimes you need to make decisions that is best for the people and not the Party even if it means that your party will alienate you. Mbeki took that risk and was alienated but if the ANC supported his decision, our political and economic situation would have been so different and so much better.

Despite his aversion to taking bold and unpopular decisions, I believe that President Ramaphosa is the right leader to move South Africa forward, but he just needs to have a stronger will and believe in himself. Mr President do the right thing, follow your heart and moral compass.

Will the ANC still lead after the May 2019 elections?

My prediction is that the ANC will win the 2019 elections. My advice to Ramaphosa is to make the unpopular decision and get rid of all the people that are bringing the ANC and our country down. Get rid of the members that are using the ANC as a vehicle to further their own corrupt personal agenda which I am sure goes against the true vision of the Party. Get rid of incompetent people whose decisions are costing South Africa dearly. This may drastically reduce the power base of the ANC but not to the extent that will cost the ANC the election after that. Once the deadwood ministers are disposed of, the ANC should regroup and follow their original vision to create a truly non-racial, united and democratic rainbow nation.

Mandela's Government of National Unity included incumbents from other political parties. With the likes of F. W. de Klerk, Derek Keys, Chief Mangosuthu Buthelezi, Roelf Meyer and Pik Botha in the Cabinet, the ANC showed a strong commitment to a united democratic South Africa. So committed was Mandela to this vision that he even appointed Chris Liebenberg to succeed Finance Minister Derek Keys in September 1994 even though he was not affiliated to any political party. My advice to Ramaphosa is to follow Mandela's strategy and include members of other political parties in his Cabinet. This inclusivity will force the opposition to get involved and take ownership of solving the current problems in South Africa as opposed to standing on the side lines and criticising the efforts of the Ruling Party. We need everyone irrespective of political affiliation to be involved and get South Africa out of this economic abyss. I personally would like to see the opposition Parties playing a more constructive role in making South Africa a better place instead of their current watchdog strategy of criticising every move of the ANC.

The Ruling Party has the potential of getting South Africa back on track, but it will need a lot of support from the people and it needs to work with and not against the opposition parties. I think the ANC is still a very arrogant party. They have yet to publicly apologise for giving us Jacob Zuma - not for one term but for almost two terms, state capture and E-tolls. The leadership under Ramaphosa condemns corruption and state capture as if they had nothing to do with it. The justice system to deal with corruption has been compromised and to date no one has been charged with these atrocities. The corrupt beneficiaries of state capture are still enjoying their ill-gotten gains while the poor people of South Africa suffer daily. Zuma, the architect of our country's mayhem is still campaigning for the ANC for the 2019 election. He is still a face of the ANC. But are the Opposition Parties any better?

CHAPTER 2: WHAT ABOUT THE OPPOSITION PARTIES?

T HE OPPOSITION PARTIES HAVE DONE A VERY GOOD JOB of trying to keep the ANC in check. However, in their blinkered mission to criticise every move of the Ruling Party, they have forgotten about the people who voted them in. Even their watchdog approach could not stop the widespread and blatant corruption in the Zuma Government. It is easy to criticise the ANC – Actually Zuma made it that easy by giving them enough ammunition. But to date none of the Opposition Parties have come up with realistic and workable solutions to seriously get South Africa back on track within the constraint of the ANC Ruling Party. The fact that they do not have the majority does not mean that they should forget about the promises they made to those people that voted for them. Let's compare the previous election manifestos of the two major opposition parties to see what they have achieved. Let's start with the Democratic Alliance (DA) and then the Economic Freedom Fighters (EFF).

Has the DA delivered on its promises?

It is evident that since the 1994 elections, Race is still a determinant of the way people vote. The DA is still considered the party of choice among White, Indian and Coloured voters. It is estimated that in the 2014 elections, the DA secured almost an overwhelming majority of the White vote and most of the Indian and Coloured votes. This creates a perception that the DA is not an option for most Black voters especially in the townships and rural areas. Be that as it may, what has the DA done for these voters?

If we look at the priorities of the DA in their 2014 election manifesto, we find that the DA intended to eradicate corruption, fast track service delivery, have accountable parliamentary ministers, create safer communities, fight gangsterism and drugs, introduce good affordable health, increase social grants to a living standard and speed up land reform. These priorities on paper are applaudable but it appears that these priorities were contingent upon the DA winning the 2014 elections and the 22.23% of people that voted for them did so in vain. If we take just one priority that the DA should have delivered on, I posit that it would be fighting gangsterism and drugs. Cape Town is a city where gangsterism is rife and the situation is out of control. The DA has enjoyed a majority win of Cape Town for most of the democratic era and has done very little to curb the scourge of gangsterism.

The DA has forgotten all about its 2014 election promises and has become a toothless watchdog to the ANC Government. Everything that it does revolves around the shortcomings of the ANC. Even its 2019 National electioneering is about the failings of the ANC and it uses tragedies like the Life Esidimeni debacle to get votes. This is so sick and nothing that the DA says in defense of this advert creates an honest, warm feeling about this Party. As a voter I do not feel confident that this Party truly has my best interests in mind or even understands my needs. I get the feeling that they have a narrow mindset in that they have accepted the reality that they will not win the coming National elections of 2019 and are only looking to maximise their seats in parliament. They are not serious about moving our country forward and uniting the people of South Africa. Their leader, Mmusi Maimane appears to be just a poster child to get the much-needed Black urban votes. If given proper autonomy, Maimane's true leadership will probably take this party forward to realise its real potential. This is unlikely to happen before the 2019 National elections.

Has the EFF delivered on its promises?

The EFF positioned itself as a new opposition party that stood alongside the poor Black majority and against corruption. The unpopularity of Jacob Zuma and the lack of effort in addressing the glaring rural social and economic problems created the environment that supported a shift in the political dynamics at the polls. There was a feeling of discontent amongst the large populous of young and poor voters who felt abandoned by the ANC but could not vote for the "White" DA. This provided a fertile platform for the emergence of a new political party offering different solutions, adopting a radical approach and most importantly, targeted the burning issues of these groups. Julius Malema and his EFF ascended as the Political Party that represented the poor turning all their concerns into a radical, rigid and pro-poor operation by highlighting their frustration and advancing their cause. The EFF positioned themselves by filling the gap in the political arena and disrupting the status quo. They offered a new and alternative approach by being the voice of the voiceless and challenged the ANC's democratic, social and economic ideologies.

The EFF's branding bears a resemblance to a new consumer product offering with mass appeal. Their use of the revolutionary red colour is a symbolic stroke of genius highlighting the plight of the poor. This target population identifies with the EFF brand and sees this Party as being one of them. In branding themselves as the voice of poor and young Black South Africans, they have alienated many disillusioned people from other race groups who are also looking for an alternative Party. Julius Malema has publicly denounced Whites and Indians as racist and has labelled most Coloureds as being more White than Black. In doing so the EFF has missed an opportunity to get a bigger slice of the political pie.

The focus of the EFFs 2014 election manifesto revolved around seven cardinal pillars.   These pillars were essentially the expropriation of land without compensation; nationalisation of mines, banks, and other strategic economic sectors without compensation; building government capacity; free education, healthcare and housing; job sustainability with minimum wages to bridge the income gap between the rich and the poor; development of the African economy by moving from reconciliation to justice for Africa and creating an accountable and corrupt-free government. Although they have made some inroads in getting the ANC to support land expropriation without compensation, the rest has fallen by the wayside. There have been allegations that they may have shared in the spoils of the now defunct and corrupt VBS Mutual bank. So much so for fighting corruption. Apart from making a lot of noise and playing the disruption political game, this Party does not have much to offer. Unless they become mature and take their conviction of fighting for the young and poor more seriously and become more inclusive towards other race groups, they are likely to remain just a radical opposition Party that makes a lot of noise.

So, what's the alternative?

The 2019 National Elections will be one of the most important elections since 1994. Yet many South African's are in a quandary as to which Party to vote for. None of the Parties have really delivered on their promises. I look at the behaviour of the

Political Parties and all I see is a bunch of opponents fighting to get into the parliamentary arena. We are just the pawns that they are using to get there. None of these Parties really understand or even care what we really need and want in our daily lives. This is just a sport to them and we are sponsoring them whether we like it or not.

Even Patricia de Lille's new Good Party does not give voters an alternative. It is obvious from the recent launch of their election manifesto that they have missed a huge opportunity. They have a fixation with urbanisation and improving cities and their infrastructures. Their belief is to upgrade the cities to accommodate the influx of people from the rural areas. What this Party fails to realise is that if we grow the economy in the rural areas, there will be no need for this urban migration. There is a huge economic disparity between the urban and rural regions and this needs to be addressed to ensure true economic equality between all the people of South Africa. People in rural areas should not feel disadvantaged when compared to their urban counterparts just because opportunities in their areas are non-existent.

I foresee an increase in spoiled ballots at the 2019 National Elections reflecting the disillusionment of many ordinary, hardworking South Africans.

I challenge each opposition Political Party to truly demonstrate what they are really made of. Instead of launching their election manifestos outlining eccentric promises that may be realised if they become the Ruling Party, why not do something different – something truly honest. I challenge them to adopt a poor rural area and build a microcosm of what they envisage South Africa to be if they were in charge. I challenge them to use their sponsorships to build proper housing, schools and infrastructures. They should use this project as their manifesto for sustainable economic growth where the people can flourish and be part of the larger economy. If I see this honest commitment, I will truly believe in their capabilities and I will gladly vote for any one of them. This will be hard work especially in the situation we currently find ourselves.

CHAPTER 3: WHAT IS THE CURRENT SITUATION?

T HE ZUMA REGIME HAS LEFT MANY SOUTH AFRICANS with a sad feeling of betrayal by a Government they trusted. The politicians' have only shown interest in winning and rescinded on delivering on their promises post elections. This pain is deeply embedded in the souls of the people reflecting a perceived sense of hopelessness. We have witnessed to the opulence of Zuma's political elites and alleged business partners. We watched our democracy being exploited to the benefit of Zuma, his family, corrupt officials and those with close ties to him. This devastation has left South Africa with a sluggish economy, VAT (value added tax) increase, increased crime and unemployment and continued poverty.

Poverty in South Africa is ubiquitous. Unemployment, hunger and malnutrition, poor health, inadequate housing, shacks and unsafe neighbourhoods bear testament to this. This social discrimination and exclusion are also evidenced by poor infrastructure in poor communities, lack or limited access to basic services and education. The uneven distribution of resources has to some extent contributed to the high poverty levels. Poverty is a major cause of social ills such as theft, drug trafficking, gangsterism etc. and these disparities threaten to divide our nation even further. The poor distribution of wealth fuels anger and violence among the poor communities. Many children in these communities are unable to regularly attend school and fail to see a way to improve their lives as they witness their parents unable to support them. These children are forced to leave school and work to help their struggling parents with additional income perpetuating this vicious cycle.

If you ask anyone in South Africa if it is morally justifiable for someone to die from hunger or cold or extreme poverty, they would surely say no. In South Africa there exists a dichotomy of extremely wealthy people - so wealthy that it is impossible to envisage that they are living right beside people with extreme poverty and suffering. The bizarre fact is that we live in a in a country where approximately more than half the population is poor with around 25% of the poor living in extreme poverty trying to survive on an average of less than a R20 a day. The minimum wage of R3500 per month is still a slave wage and is unlikely to make a substantial difference in the lives of the poor. Social grants for the vulnerable is still sitting at a measly average of R50 per day and in many households, this is the sole income.

The reality is that people especially children are dying from hunger and lack of the necessities of life. The current solutions have simply not been able to provide everybody with the bare necessities. This suffering in my opinion is caused by a faulty socio-economic system which is materially based and benefits only a small section of society namely the wealthy and privileged. This perpetuates the reality of the poor majority. Let's unpack this nightmarish absurdity. Let's start with the unemployment in South Africa.

What is the state of unemployment?

One of the most visible forms of unemployment is the daily realism of people standing by the side of a road hoping for any job that might be offered to them. Another reality is men, women and children begging for food or any monetary relief at intersections. The legacy of apartheid that left most of its citizens with poor education and training contributing to South Africa's high unemployment rate after 1994. Apartheid orchestrated the deliberate exclusion of Black people from quality and skilled education forcing South Africa play educational catch up with most of its citizens. There is a shortage of skilled labour and a surplus of unskilled labour. This labour market has become chronically mismatched and reducing this gap should eventually reduce the rate of unemployment. However, the unemployment challenge continues to plague South Africa as unemployment progressively increases with this diminished level of education. The current educational system has not changed much from the apartheid system and is not geared to produce the relevant skills for the labour market.

South Africa's current unemployment rate has risen more than 27% with youth (15-34 years old) unemployment being the most vulnerable at around 38%. These statistics indicate that unemployment is a major problem and that Government is not doing enough to create jobs. South Africans are getting frustrated and are constantly complaining about the lack of job creation and service delivery. They believe that they voted for a better life in the first democratic election of 1994, but this has not materialised. This is evident in the form of the numerous protests on service delivery and against self-serving, uncaring and corrupt leaders of local and national Government.

Unemployment is a contributor to the many challenges we face and is associated with crime, deplorable living conditions, physical and mental wellbeing and the performance of the economy. I submit that with the widespread poverty and unemployment, people are vulnerable to criminal activities. Reducing poverty will therefore go a long way to reducing these negative effects and will positively improve the quality of life for the citizens of South Africa.

Our economy has for many reasons been unable to respond to the ever-increasing demand and sustainably of new job creation. Also, people who have been previously employed are now finding themselves without employment because of the current economic climate. Similarly, the rise in unemployment can be attributed to the failure of the informal sector to provide alternative sustainable employment. Our informal sector has grown marginally, especially in the rural areas, and is unable to absorb the snowballing unskilled labour supply. Technological advancements that replace unskilled labour with automated systems, have also played a key role in reducing opportunities for employing unskilled manual labourers. The obvious solution is to produce a more skilled and semi-skilled employable workforce, but our current education system does not support this. Let's unpack the state of our education system.

What is the state of our education?

To obtain a full grasp of where South Africa is with its education system today, it is pertinent to understand the education system in the apartheid era. During apartheid, the Bantu Education Act (No. 47) of 1953 created a chasm in educational opportunities for the different racial groups in South Africa. This act stated that learners of different races were not allowed to study in the same schools. It banned the inclusion of mathematics and science in the curriculum of the Black education system as there was a belief that these subjects were not necessary. The young Black South Africans were groomed for highly physical, low-wage labour. It also protected the privileged White minority group from competition in the skilled labour force.

Educational funding and resources for Whites was the highest whereas the funding and resources allocated to Black education were minimal in comparison. Schools for Black children had inferior facilities and were often without text books. Teachers had basic or poor professional qualifications. There was a significant disparity in teacher and learner ratio with an average in a "White" primary school being one teacher to eighteen learners as opposed to the estimated one teacher to thirty-nine learners in "Black" primary schools. In my primary school we were forty learners in the class. Most of all teachers in "White" schools had professional teaching qualifications while a minority of teachers in "Black" schools were qualified.

One of the first changes made to the education system in the early 1990s was the traditional "White" schools being re-classified as Model B schools permitting limited access to children of other races with preference given to children living within the area of the school. However, in the dying days of apartheid, most White public schools were changed to semi-private Model C schools. This meant that the school was given the right to appoint teachers, decide on admission policies and impose fees. The financing and control of the apartheid "White" schools became the responsibility of the "White" parents in the form of School Governing Bodies.

Addressing these past injustices in our education system would have been one of the most horrendous tasks of our current government. Nowadays every South African has the right to basic education, as well as to further their education. This was set out in the 1996 Bill of Rights as contained in our Constitution. Government is mandated to make education available and accessible to all South Africans and educational policies have since been rewritten with the purpose of ensuring an equal, and quality education for all South Africans. So, in the last 25 years, how far have we come?

All restrictions on racial integration in schools were officially abolished post-apartheid. The 1996 South African Schools Act outlined most of the financing and governance requirements in Model C and Public schools. The National Norms and Standards for School Funding Policy was published in 1998. This policy effectively sought to reallocate funds equitably resulting in the poorest and neediest schools receiving a higher allocation of funding per learner. The semi-independent Model C schools receives a lump sum of money from the Government. The School Governing Body is given the authority to allocate this money and resources. These schools tend to charge school fees generating additional funding that allows them to employ more teachers, maintain buildings and cover costs that exceed Government funding. In contrast, Public schools receive all their funding from Government. It is Government that regulates how these funds are spent. They are not allowed to charge school fees and are unable to employ additional teachers over and above the Government allocation. The aim of this policy is to ensure that the poorer students have access to education, regardless of their parents' financial situation. Most of the Public schools are found in the previous Black, and rural areas. The estimated post-apartheid teacher learner ratio in these schools is one teacher to thirty-five learners. There has been no improvement from the oppressive apartheid era.

The implementation of the no fee policy for the poorest schools was meant to reduce the inequalities in the public schooling system. The policy assumes that by allocating more money to these schools, the conditions of these schools will improve. The assumption of this scenario being that schools would utilise the money wisely in line with Government's vision to redress the educational inequalities. Another assumption is that there would be no problems regarding how the schools use public money and that schools would not be guilty of fruitless and wasteful expenditure. The no fee school policy is deemed to promote accountability, transparency and responsibility for the sake of the children.

The reality is that knowledge of sound financial management practices is essential when spending school money and unfortunately this is lacking in the Governing Bodies of many no fee schools. There is little or no training support from Government in this regard. So even though many schools are spending the school funds properly according to the applicable rules and regulations, a significant number of schools spend the money in ways that do not benefit the learners. Instead they tend to engage in illegal activities that contravene the applicable rules and regulations.

Although Government's allocation of more money and resources to the poorest and neediest schools was theoretically a feasible solution, nothing much has changed since the pre-democracy early 1990's. Schools in poor and rural areas are still poorly equipped and the standard of education is inferior to the previously "White" Public schools. The so-called Model C schools are now dotted with a few Black learners creating an illusion of Democracy. Good education is critical for increasing our economy and with our current education system basically mirroring that of the apartheid system and denying quality education to most of the learners, we are far from addressing this inequality.

Despite the 25 years of democracy, Bantu education is still alive and flourishing in the Black and the rural areas. Take a recent example of the Myolwa Primary School in Lusikisiki where learners are forced to learn in mud structures and under trees. There are in the region of 110 learners in a single classroom. The cherry on the top is the alleged four million nine hundred thousand rand spent by Government for nine basic toilets. These toilets are still not completed. The fact is that with this money you could have built an entire classroom block with toilets makes this project cost inconceivable. This smells of yet another corrupt transaction with the poor learners being the unfortunate victims. It could also be incompetent Government officials with no clue as to what they should be doing. There is probably a "Steve Jobs" in a poor or rural Public school waiting for the right support, opportunity and encouragement to achieve his or her dream. Such talent is currently being overlooked and the tragedy is that we could use any visionary support to get out of our current situation.

A good education system encourages learners to think in an entrepreneurial way, build small businesses or even venture and create new industries. Coupled with a good education is a nurturing home environment for our youth to flourish. How does the housing situation compare?

What is the state of free housing for the poor?

Most Governments including South Africa, are convinced that owning a house is the right way to go. It is estimated that 6% of our working population bring home less than R1 000 a month with some families living off a measly R345 a month. An estimated two-thirds of the population are forced to manage with an average of R 1 800 per month making it impossible to buy a house or obtain bank loans. This creates an overwhelming need for government intervention. The free housing program introduced in 1994 was intended to be the answer to the housing crisis. The construction of these houses was heralded as an important measure of restoring the dignity of the poor and a victory for democratic South Africa. It was envisioned that the mass provision of free housing would alleviate vagrancy, reduce informal housing and create social upliftment through the pride of home ownership.

Unfortunately, the poor execution of this policy, corruption and theft resulted in poor building standards with serious defects emerging in many houses. Instead of improving the lives of the poor and eradicating poverty, the chief beneficiaries of this initiative were the emerging contractors and corrupt officials. These houses, built in the historically disadvantaged areas, are very small with no partitioning. Families are virtually living in a single room like the informal housing. The new homeowner is also given a further burden to maintain their new asset – an additional cost they cannot afford as their main priority is providing food. What was intended to be a positive initiative by Government has turned out to be a nightmare for the intended recipients because of the shoddy implementation and corruption.

Government needs to revisit the current free housing policies, programs and implementation methods. What is needed is amendments to these policies to provide housing that will improve the quality of life for the poor. This should be done in consultation with all stakeholders including the recipients. Tapping into the wealth of knowledge of academia and successes in other countries can contribute to this process. What should inform the policy changes is the actual needs of the recipients. Do they have a preference to renting a house as opposed to owning it? Are there other models that can be looked at? Is there an interim structured solution that can reduce the hazards of informal housing and give people a safe and secure place to stay until a free house is allocated to them? How can the corruption be eradicated?

With housing still in a crisis, how is our heath care systems holding out?

What is the state of our health care?

In 1994 our Government inherited a highly fragmented and bureaucratic public health system that provided services in line with the discriminatory apartheid policies. Health services for Whites were more accessible and better than those for Blacks. Access to health services in the rural areas were more challenging compared to the urban areas.

Fortunately, in democratic South Africa, the right of every citizen to access health care services is mandatory. This is penned in Section 27 of the Constitution and is one of the socio-economic rights that is protected. The White Paper for the Transformation of the Health Sector in South Africa was released in April 1997. This was a significant attempt to correct the past by creating a unified but decentralised National Health System. This was deemed to be the most appropriate vehicle for the delivery of Public Health care to all. However, it is evident that the efforts of Government to improve access to health care services have not translated to the entitlements of these rights to all South Africans.

Although the Health Department has compiled progressive policies and legislative frameworks to access health care services, there are huge gaps in the implementation of these policies and legislation. These include an insufficient capacity of qualified staff to offer health care services and limited health care services to the poor and rural areas. The unequal implementation and monitoring of policies have perpetuated massive health inequalities in the public health sector. These inequalities are evident between provinces, the public and private sector and the rich and the poor. So much for our constitutional commitment to ensure that all have access to health care services. The lack of health care transformation raises doubts as to whether the Government has pro-actively complied with its constitutional mandate to prevent inequality in accessing health care services. Nothing much has improved since the apartheid era.

Health care facilities in poor and rural areas still pose perpetual problems. The harrowing example of the Life Esidimeni debacle bears testament to the crisis in our public health care system. In Gugulethu, a seventeen-month baby died on his grandmother's back after the grandmother was turned away from three different public health care facilities. She was turned away from Nyanga Clinic because they had reached the daily quota for treating sick children. The child was then taken to Gugulethu Maternal Obstetrics Unit (MOU) and was refused access by security because the facility did not offer services to sick children. In desperation, the grandmother went to Gugulethu Community Health Clinic (CHC). After waiting for more than two hours she was told to come the following day as the nurses had reached their daily quota of sick children. The child sadly died while being carried on his grandmother's back during their two-hour walk home. The Rahima Moosa Mother and Child Hospital is another example where nine new born babies died following a necrotising enterocolitis bacterial outbreak. A teenager gave birth on the pavement outside the MOU facility in Gugulethu just hours after being discharged on the assumption that she was not in labour. Sadly, the security staff refused to let her back into the premises and the nurses refused to help her as they claimed it was not their problem because it had happened outside hospital.

These are only a few of the heart-breaking incidents reflecting the sad state of our Public Health Care Facilities. The lack of morality amongst the medical personnel is omnipresent. Understandably, this has given rise to malpractice litigation against the Health Ministry taking the focus off the constitutional commitment to providing primary health care to all. It is estimated that just the Gauteng Health Department alone is facing ligation to the value of twenty-two billion rand. This money would obviously be better spent on improving the current primary health services as opposed to paying copious amounts of money in compensation for incompetence. Doing it right first time is always the best.

South Africa's health care system is also riddled by political influence. The Minister of Health who heads up the health care system is a political appointment reporting to the President. The two provincial heads of health care consist of the

MEC (Member of the Executive Council) for health, a political appointment, and the Superintendent General, a clinical appointment. The political appointments have immense power over the direction in which health care services are driven and this power is detrimental of the people of South Africa. The apartheid era bears testament to the ills of its political influences that guaranteed the minority group the best health care at the expense of the majority. It pains me to ask the worrying questions – Is our health care system driven by political influence? Should decisions in a highly specialised field like medicine be allowed to be overridden by our politicians and corruption? Where to from here?

The entire Public Health Care System needs a complete overhaul. The National Health Insurance (NHI) is touted as the "silver bullet" to all the problems in Public Health Care. The reality is that the existing system needs to be cleaned up first before we look at major changes. The NHI will not magically eradicate the current problems and deliver quality primary health care to all. We need to remove the political interference and leave it to the relevant professionals to restore this failed system.

What is the state of crime and corruption?

Crime is recognised as one of the most difficult challenges in post-apartheid South Africa. Violent crime such as murder, assault, gang violence, organised crime and femicide is particularly prevalent in South Africa. There are also crimes relating to property such as burglaries and vehicle thefts. Crime statistics do not fully represent all crime in South Africa as many individuals do not report crimes due to their lack of faith in the police and NPA (National Prosecuting Authority). There is a strong perception amongst South Africans that the police, the NPA together with other organs of the State is captured by corrupt criminals. Unfortunately, our judicial system is so clogged up with prosecuting violent criminals that it is unable to function speedily and efficiently. This creates a utopian environment for bribery and corruption to thrive.

South Africa has one of the highest reported crime statistics in the world. The Zuma regime is responsible for increased socioeconomic factors such as unemployment and the widespread level of income inequality which play an important role in these crime statistics. High levels of unemployment in a low economic growth situation imply that there is a low probability of gaining a legal income thereby increasing the opportunity cost of criminal activity. South Africa has one of the highest unemployment rates in the world. There is no doubt that a significant number of citizens are struggling to meet their basic survival needs. Inequality in South Africa is also exceptionally high and given these socioeconomic conditions, our crime rate statistics are no surprise.

Our Constitution clearly states that, in Public Administration, a high standard of professional ethics must be promoted and maintained. The South African Police Service's (SAPS) Code of Conduct (1997) states that "the police service should work actively towards preventing any form of corruption and bringing those guilty of unethical conduct to justice". The Service Integrity Framework of the SAPS Strategic Plan Document (2002/5) encourages police officers to resist and expose any form of unethical conduct. Every police officer should therefore exhibit a high level of professional ethics when providing safety and security services to the public. Despite these policies, there is an increasing level of unethical behaviours amongst our police officers. This lack of accountability together with corrupt practices has become so prevalent resulting in an ethical crisis in the police force. Brazen unethical practices such as outright bribery, corruption and abuse of public property, are impeding ethical behaviour in our police force. This has reduced the public's confidence in the police force creating an environment for criminals to operate with impunity knowing they can get away with anything.

It is the honest, law abiding citizens of South Africa that are paying the ultimate price as we live in daily fear of our lives. A father accidently shot and killed his sixteen-year-old son in a school carpark as he thought he was being hijacked. A Soweto school security guard was acquitted of three counts of rape and eleven counts of sexual assault because of the sloppy way in which the case was handled by the police and the prosecution. This resulted in the inability of the prosecution to provide proper supporting evidence. There is no will and urgency for the "Law and Order" public servants to do their jobs effectively and constitutionally. Whether they do their job or not, they will still receive a salary at the end of the month and no punitive action will be taken against them for non-performance. Who is responsible for this malady eroding any goodwill in our police force? I believe it's our politicians who are the real culprits.

In South Africa, there is a progressive blurring of the lines between the criminal and noncriminal behaviour and this can be attributed to our political landscape becoming interconnected with crime. The weakness and greed in our previous president have for years provided the perfect conditions for the growth of organised crime, corruption and state capture. Our law enforcement agencies, judicial and prison systems are understaffed and underfunded having outdated or non-functional equipment and procedures. This has created an opportunistic environment for criminals and state officials to exploit. Nepotism, corruption and patronage has been the order of the day under the Zuma regime resulting in a weakened Government that lacked the capacity to keep its citizens safe. The Zuma regime accordingly became a criminal enterprise accumulating power through corrupt activities and appointing toothless state officials in crime fighting positions. This Government reflected a low level of state legitimacy, ineffective rules that worked against serving public interest, and an ineffective and captured criminal justice system.

This devastation cannot be cleaned up and rebuilt overnight as we methodically attempt to correct this calamity and remove criminals from our State. Crime and corruption must go if we are serious about rebuilding South Africa from the ashes of Zuma destruction.

I have only highlighted some of the key issues that are preventing growth and development in South Africa. The current situation is dire and appears to be hopeless. But I feel that amidst all this devastation, is room for a total overhaul of our current systems giving rise to a new structure that will give our country a totally democratic, non-corrupt people's country that will be a beacon for the rest of the world to emulate. Is it doable? Let's find out.

CHAPTER 4: IS SOUTH AFRICA POISED FOR A NEW BEGINNING? WHAT BEGINNING? HOW REALISTIC?

T HE ROAD TO RECOVERY SEEMS ALMOST IMPOSSIBLE...or is it? To truly eliminate poverty and make South Africa truly democratic, we need a different but more positive mindset. Let's unpack this further.

South Africa as a large Corporation

If we viewed South Africa as a large corporation as opposed to another global political player, the citizens would be the equivalent of shareholders and Government the executive team managing their investment. We could then apply the principles of business rescue to fix the problems. Business rescue in a nutshell is a formal process that focuses on companies in financial distress bringing them back to wealth status. The key to business rescue success is to have a solid turnaround strategy and plan. A competent team to implement this plan is critical. In the spirit of business rescue, I would suggest putting together a core team of multidisciplinary specialists including business rescue practitioners to develop a rescue plan to bring our country out of this quagmire. Treating South Africa as a business removes all the political emotions and instead creates an objective and implementable solution.

Let's face it, contrary to what politicians are spinning, South Africa like any other country is just a big organisation owned by the people who live in it. The role of Government is to increase value to the people who elected them. Despite the current Government culpability in the current situation, they cannot reverse this damage alone. We desperately need a different approach to move forward. We need an approach that would dilute the power of the Government and give it back to the people. The role of Government should be supportive with the interest of the people being its main priority. This also means that the people cannot sit back and wait for Government to do the right thing, we all need to get involved in the solution. Let's apply this principle to the Eskom debacle.

Load shedding has reared its ugly head again. Eskom is in a severe crisis with a huge debt burden of R420 billion. Critics are saying that Eskom is technically insolvent and is unlikely to survive beyond April 2019. The demise of Eskom would be a catastrophe and we cannot let this happen. The design flaws of the Medupi and Kusile Power Stations are the main reason why they are not functioning optimally. The suboptimal boiler specifications and shoddy installations by Hitachi Africa has worsened this crisis. The ANC's Chancellor House has a stake in Hitachi Africa and we can surmise that the decision to give the contract to Hitachi Africa was a political one. This decision has sadly ensured that we experience load shedding yet again. The moral action by the ANC would be to get Chancellor House to pay for the new design and rectifications at the Medupi and Kusile Power Stations.

Cyril Ramaphosa's plan to unbundle Eskom should happen sooner than later. When this happens, it is imperative that business rescue practitioners drive this unbundling process. The Labour Unions are not supporting this unbundling process because they are protecting the jobs of the overly inflated workforce at Eskom. Unfortunately, jobs will have to go to keep the lights on. How should Cyril Ramaphosa deal with this dilemma?

Life is about comprises and with the crisis at Eskom, there should be comprises. I understand why the Labour Unions are taking this stance. The paradox of massive job losses amidst the corrupt and incompetent Ministers in Parliament sitting back and earning a huge salary with perks. As a comprise, I personally challenge Cyril Ramaphosa to reduce his presidential salary to R1 per annum. In solidarity with this gesture, he should cut the salaries of all the Cabinet Ministers and Deputies by at least 50%. I am sure after doing this the Labour Unions will be more willing to come to the party and resolve the Eskom crisis. If I was Cyril Ramaphosa, I would also freeze all new appointments in other Government departments and offer these positions first to the affected Eskom employees. This would drastically reduce the amount of retrenchments. This is typically what an organisation in crisis and under business rescue would do.

Despite who is responsible for the Eskom crisis, it affects everyone. If Cyril Ramaphosa and his Ministers take a salary cut to help Eskom, I will personally offer my services pro bono to help fix Eskom. I challenge every South African to do the same if possible. I challenge the Engineering Council of South Africa and the South African Institute of Electrical Engineers to pool together their expertise and get Eskom back on track. I challenge the Engineering departments of all Academic institutions to use their knowledge to help solve Eskom's problems. Do this because you care for South Africa and not for monetary rewards. Do this because we should not let corruption cripple our country. Together we can save Eskom in a truly democratic way.

Meeting the minimum requirements of the People

In the spirit of solidarity, we need a progressive system that provides practical and compassionate solutions to our current economic and social problems. We need a system that will guarantee the minimum requirements of life with increased monetary capacity of all citizens. We need a truly democratic economic system. Our rescue plan should be informed by the needs of the people as opposed to the perceived needs of the people as determined by the politicians.

The minimum requirements of life are food, shelter, clothing, education, health care and security. If these requirements are guaranteed to every citizen of South Africa, nobody will have to worry about going hungry, ill health, basic and tertiary education for their children, losing their job or having a safe place to stay. This liberation would mean that people will not live in fear for their daily survival. They would see that their future is getting better, resulting in an improvement in their quality of life.

To move forward, we first need to guarantee the minimum requirements to all South Africans and secondly, create a sustainable environment for individual wealth accumulation. This can be achieved by creating pockets of decentralised community-based economies that allow for small scale private enterprises to flourish through instruments such as Cooperatives. This would give communities the power to decide their own economic future instead of Government making the decisions for them. South Africa is a very diverse country where the needs of one community may differ from the needs of another, therefore applying blanket policies will not completely root out poverty or give every citizen the bare requirements for life.

So where do we start? Before we look at a new way of moving forward, we need to unpack some low hanging solutions that can propel our country forward. Let's look at unemployment as an example.

Reducing the unemployment gap

Most South Africans are trapped in a downward spiraling abyss of low education and skills leading to low wages and unsecured employment. This can be attributed to the apartheid legacy and inability or lack of will of our current Government to actively make the required bold changes to move our country forward. Without a solid and steady employment and liveable wage, it is impossible for anyone to live in a decent house, have enough money for food and bare necessities and educate their children. The future generation will not realise their dreams and improve on the status quo. The obvious solution to getting out of this abyss is access to skills improvement which will result in better jobs. This in turn will provide food, shelter and education for the children, creating a positive turnaround. Despite the current situation, South Africa is poised to take its people out of this forsaken situation and we have the resources to do it. All we need now is the will, unity and patriotism of everyone and honest politicians.

South Africa is one of the wealthiest countries in the world in terms of its abundance of natural resources. South Africa is famous for mineral resources that make up a large percentage of the world's reserves. This makes it one of the most valuable countries in the world in terms of natural resources. South Africa has an estimated value of two to five trillion dollars of natural resources with platinum and manganese reserves being the largest in the world. It is also a leading producer of gold, coal, diamonds, chromite ore, iron ore, copper, silver, lead, zinc, titanium, uranium, ferrochrome and vanadium. Similarly, the United States of America (USA) has deposits of crude oil, coal, uranium, copper, silver, gold, mercury, zinc, lead, and very small amounts of diamonds and many more natural elements.

Natural resources should be considered as superior economic goods as they are not produced and will yield investments that can be a huge source of economic growth if properly managed. Both countries have rich natural resource deposits and yet the USA with this wide pool of natural resources has become a leader in the world's market driven economies. The pioneering attitude and patriotism of the people of the USA has also driven this country to succeed. The leaders of South Africa on the other hand are manipulating natural resources for their own motive and political agenda. This needs to change!

The clear lack of patriotism and clear divide amongst racial lines is hampering the potential growth of our country. Sadly, our politicians are pushing their selfish personal agenda by perpetuating the racial divide instead of uniting the citizens of South Africa. However, amidst this hopeless backdrop, there are obvious interventions that we can adopt to kickstart our economy and create more employment opportunities. We have similar resources to the USA and if they can do it, so can we. Surely this can help in reducing the unemployment gap. All we need is a pioneering and patriotic attitude.

Are there immediate interventions? The next chapters will further unpack some of these interventions. It may be a hectic read but the result will be a montage of possibilities revealing that our situation is not as hopeless as we think. There is a way forward.

CHAPTER 5: GROWING OUR CURRENT INDUSTRIES. WHAT'S STOPPING US?

S OUTH AFRICA IS ITS OWN DOOMSAYER with Government digging its grave with corruption, political mayhem, infighting and choking any real form of growth with endless red tape and incompetence. Political parties are further dividing the country with their biased narratives that encourage citizens to look at each other with suspicion, distrust and racial undertones instead of ordinary people just making a living for themselves and striving for the same purpose – living in a proudly South African country that exudes patriotism. The result is a self-fulfilling prophetic perception of another failed corrupt African country. A country with no hope of economic growth, developed country success and patriotic citizens.

On the surface we see a wrecked country in chaos. If we look beyond this bleak outlook we will see real possibilities of healing. Ironically because of this hopelessness, South Africa is well positioned to entertain the possibility of becoming a super country. After destruction, it is easier to start new and create something even greater as opposed to applying band-aids to a failing country. My submission on a totally new way of doing things will come later but for now there are many quick fixes that we can implement to get our economy moving in the right direction. We just need to collectively put our mind together and do it. I have come up with a few ideas, some more plausible than others. These include improving growth in our existing sectors and starting new ones. To illustrate this, let's discuss some of my ideas of improving growth in our existing sectors. Since South Africa has the potential of being a successful microcosm of the USA, mining is a good industry to start with.

The Mining Industry

The South African mining industry has been in a downward trajectory for at least the last decade. This industry, once the pinnacle of foreign revenues has faded. Operating costs are soaring, and it is plagued with political and regulatory interference. Unlike other business such as the opening of a retail store, a new mine is subjected to immense scrutiny from Government and the affected community.

A dioramic view of historic literature is likely to expose mining as a cornerstone of South Africa's economic history. This industry was historically built on a political society divided along racial lines and wears two hats depending on which side of the racial line the narrator is. The beneficiaries of apartheid will associate mining with industrialisation and economic development while the majority who lived on the fringes of this industry serving as labourers would associate mining with extreme poverty, underdevelopment and human rights abuse. The post-apartheid view of the industry has not changed significantly, and new policies merely act as makeshift attempts to bridge the racial divide. The platinum belt for example is still characterised by poverty and labour unrest and this pressure cooker situation exploded into the international spotlight in August 2012, when thirty-four mineworkers were killed by police during a labour strike in Marikana in the North West Province. In their grievance, this mineworking community highlighted their low wages, poor working and living conditions despite being part of this mineral enriched area.

Mining is still a major economic contributor, but this industry's beneficiaries are largely the apartheid minority and its contribution to the livelihood of the surrounding community highly contested. Post-apartheid mineral rights have been nationalised with the Government being the custodian of these rights. Despite the introduction of new policies, the industry has done little to transform. It still suffers from protracted labour strikes, community dissatisfaction and political interference. Limpopo Province for example has an abundance of natural resources with large mining operations and is ironically one of the poorest provinces in South Africa. Like Limpopo Province, mining in Rustenburg in the North West province is a major source of employment, be it directly or indirectly. However, poverty and unemployment remain high in Rustenburg. There is also a visible lack of bulk infrastructure to support development.

Mining communities are defined by an influx of low-skilled migrant workers seeking job opportunities. There are informal settlements around the mines as the living allowance provides an incentive for workers to seek alternative accommodation to mine hostels. The surrounding communities see no visible benefit from mining contradicting the mining companies' claims of substantial positive socioeconomic community initiatives.

The mining industry needs a complete overhaul to address the historic issues still hounding it. I do not have a workable solution for this industry. However, I can confidently say that to ensure mining flourishes, drastic action must be taken to fix the problems. South Africa has a long history of being a resource rich nation and this has made it one of the strongest countries in Africa. Mines, their employees and their suppliers are collectively major contributors to the economy. It is therefore critical that the mining sector be returned to profitability with major beneficiaries being its surrounding communities. The backbone of this industry is the miners and they must be treated and compensated equitably. It has the potential of growing our economy in terms of foreign investment, export markets and employment.

Tourism is another industry that has the potential of bringing wealth to South Africa but is plagued with problems. Let's take a closer look at possibilities in this industry.

The Tourism Industry

The tourism industry is multifaceted and contributes to a wide range of industries such as real estate, entertainment, events, and agriculture. It also creates prospects for entrepreneurs and employment making it a key driver for economic growth. Tourism is highly labour-intensive and is well positioned to absorb South Africa's surplus unskilled labour and generate foreign currency. Exploiting this sector will only benefit the economy.

Exploitation in this industry is sadly directed towards its employees. The tourism industry is a conduit for job opportunities especially to the youth entering the labour market for the first time. Our first democratic Government had the ambitious goal of making tourism one of the key instruments for economic expansion, job creation and foreign monetary contributions. Unfortunately, the follow through was poor and international tourist visits to South Africa has declined. This is probably due to the violent public protests, social unrest, increase in violent crime and the hostile visa regulations and applications which has only recently being lifted.

There is a skills mismatch between tourism trainees, graduates and the employers' expectations of the calibre of skilled recruits needed to move their business forward. This skills mismatch results in a high staff turnover limiting the career growth of trainees and graduates. Eventually they leave the industry because of unfulfilled expectations. Tourism is a major source of unskilled employment but challenges such as legislative compliance, poor wage offerings and seasonal work is prevalent. This exposes the industry to exploitation of vulnerable employees in the form of unfavourable working conditions. Salary levels continue to be indicative of previous racial grouping with White employees earning more compared to their Black counterparts. These challenges hamper any good intentions of driving this industry forward towards sustainable growth.

In my opinion, Government has clearly dropped the ball in this industry. It has lost out on a relatively easy way of creating employment opportunities which can ultimately improve the lives of many citizens. It is imperative that South Africa takes steps to maximise the potential value of tourism, by actively targeting and promoting this sector. Give the sector the attention that it needs, address the burning issues and the rewards will be exponential.

Tourism is one of the industries that also encourages the creation of small businesses which play a crucial role in our economy. How is this industry doing?

The Small Business Sector

In South Africa, there is a visible lack of entrepreneurship and this contributes to the high rate of unemployment. Our country remains one of the more poorly performing countries with regards to entrepreneurial activities. A large portion of people who attempt to open small businesses do not prosper as they lack the necessary entrepreneurship support. Although small and medium-sized enterprises make up about 98.5% of our economy, they have created only 28% of all jobs. If we benchmark these statistics globally, we will find that an estimated 60% to 70% of a country's workforce is employed in this sector. South Africa has fallen far behind.

One of the major inhibitors to the development of small businesses is the high taxation rate in South Africa. This greatly reduces profit incentives. The taxation costs related to VAT and company tax is among the highest in the world. The complexity of the tax system also increases the cost of doing business. Small businesses do not have the capacity to administer these tax returns and tend to outsource this to experts for an additional fee just to meet these legal requirements. Also, the presence of high levels of bureaucracy and red tape significantly increases the cost of starting a business in South Africa. This, together with having to negotiate with corrupt officials, makes the offerings of small business goods and services uncompetitive. Other barriers facing the small business sector relates to the difficulty in accessing markets and finance, restrictive labour regulations, crime and limited support infrastructure.

The vague and inconsistent definition of Government strategies for small, very small, and medium business as described in the applicable laws and regulations causes chaos in this sector. The regulatory environment is no different. There are overlapping and sometimes conflicting regulatory requirements across multiple Government departments. This together with administrative inefficiencies, poor communication and access to information imply that small business owners are spending a crazy amount of time dealing with regulatory compliance. This lack of clarity gives rise to confusion and unnecessary barriers for small businesses to flourish. The demise of small businesses fails to add any value to our failing economy.

The way forward would be to address the issues limiting its growth and bring it on par with global standards. Government can begin with creating a more attractive environment for people to enter this sector and provide incentives to boost growth. They can start with reducing regulatory, tax and red tape burdens on small businesses. This is a crucial sector and its success has the potential to catapult South Africa into one of the fastest growing global economies.

We need a more supportive Government to achieve this. Our Government needs to clean up its act and there is so many areas that can be transformed into efficient mechanisms that support growth. Government's huge property and immovable asset portfolio is a good an example. Let's examine this further.

Public Sector Property and Immovable Asset Portfolio

Government is the biggest property owner in the country but unfortunately, the returns on these assets are not in line with the capital expenditure. This is mainly due to the maladministration of the property portfolio. The National Department of Public Works (NDPW) is the custodian of this huge property portfolio. Government has a rough estimate of 250 thousand properties valued around R150 billion. It costs in the region of 15 billion rand per annum to maintain them. The NDPW are unable to effectively manage this portfolio. Key strategic decisions lie with the executive made up of politicians who lack the technical knowledge and expertise. These politicians can sadly override property management decisions proposed by the professionals. The Nkandla debacle is a good example of a politically corrupt agenda trumping sensible professional advice and submissions. Land and property ownership are currently a hot topic and amidst this debate I question whether Government really knows what properties and immovable assets it owns, the condition of these assets, the current use of these assets and the value of these assets.

Strategic property management relates to matters of procurement, maintenance, disposal of surplus property assets and understanding the asset life cycle. Ideally Government should have a system in place to manage this portfolio. The identification and inventory of property and immovable assets, its control, and administration is the cornerstone of a proper asset management system. Asset registers and management systems provide valuable information about the assets with respect to their maintenance requirements, financial and operational management. The requirement for a comprehensive asset register in the public sector can never be over emphasised, as this forms the backbone of any property portfolio. It essentially provides valuable information that Government could use to implement the best property management practices.

Let's face it, Government needs property to offer effective and efficient services to the public, thereby fulfilling its social and welfare obligations. Lack of proper management has created a tension between Government and the citizens using its facilities. This inefficient management of the property portfolio plus incompetent and corrupt political appointees has resulted in dodgy construction projects and under-utilisation of its assets. There is a distinct lack of any form of strategic approach to managing this humongous portfolio. As a result, we have poorly maintained public buildings and shoddy delivery of basic services to the people of South Africa. This is illustrated in the roof collapse at Charlotte Maxeke hospital in Johannesburg. The devastating fire at the Bank of Lisbon building in Johannesburg spiralled out of control because of non-compliance and health and safety problems. Three fire fighters lost their lives because of this. The irony is that Government is the custodian of compliance policies relating to building and people safety, yet it blatantly ignores these policies and puts the lives of its citizens in danger. In response to these tragedies, Government is notorious for cosmetic interventions by setting up board of inquiries and compiling investigative reports that are rarely followed up and eventually ignored and shelved.

Government has challenges in implementing proper planned property maintenance programs. Furthermore, it has difficulties in financial management, performance evaluation and the management of its end users. The end users are the people for example using a hospital facility or other government departments. These problems emanate from the reactive and crisis approach to managing the property portfolio, conflicting political interests, lack of strategic facilities management protocols and systems which ultimately worsen the situation. The result is a fragmented approach to managing this portfolio. Inherent inconsistencies in the general administration and vague audits that lack any material benefit are ubiquitous. There is a poor relationship between financial and asset management improvements, transparency and accountability. Major challenges are the lack of accountability by senior officials, unnecessary political interference, poor financial analysis and control and a lack of long-term planning.

Despite this bleak outlook, I believe that there is a genuine opportunity to restructure this portfolio to incorporate the best practice principles present in the private sector. The property sector, specifically Facilities Management creates both skilled and unskilled jobs and if managed properly and strategically, Government can use this platform to employ unskilled labour creating a career path for them. To make this possible, all political appointments in senior management positions in NDPW must be replaced with competent professional people who will be motivated to restructure this portfolio making it effective and efficient. There are competent professionals in South Africa with international quality credentials that can add value to this portfolio. It will also stand Government in good stead if it partners with professional bodies such as the South African Facilities Management Association (SAFMA) and the South African Property Owners Association (SAPOA).

These are only a few examples of existing industries and portfolios that can be repositioned for sustainable growth. I am sure that you may have other examples too. These interventions can be applied by improving on the status quo and positively influencing our current economic situation. New industries and initiatives must also be explored to create more jobs and increase our economic footprint. Let's look at some of the new industries that we can tap into and what's stopping us.

CHAPTER 6: PIONEERING INTO NEW INDUSTRIES. WHAT'S STOPPING US?

I N THE PREVIOUS CHAPTER I looked at a few industries to illustrate easy fixes that can boost our economy. Another area that can be explored are new industries. Introducing a new industry will likely increase employment and make South Africa more attractive for investment. One of these industries is surprisingly, the hemp industry.

Industrial Hemp Farming

In September 2018 the use of marijuana, a highly addictive strain of the cannabis plant, was decriminalised for private use. Ironically, until recently, it was illegal to cultivate hemp, a non-addictive variety of the cannabis plant, as it is classified under the cannabis species. Hemp like marijuana is cannabis. Cannabis is a species of a plant which has many different strains. The cannabis strain called marijuana is high in "delta-9-tetrahydrocannabinol (THC). This THC is what makes marijuana highly addictive. THC is the primary active component of the marijuana strain of cannabis and produces an assortment of biological and behavioural responses if consumed.

Cannabis also has a strain referred to as hemp. Hemp is farmed for industrial use and does not have addictive properties. Unlike marijuana, hemp has less than 0.3 percent THC which makes it non-addictive. The confusion between marijuana and hemp happened in the 1970s, when former USA President Nixon approved the Controlled Substances Act of 1970 to declare war on drugs. This law unintentionally outlawed hemp which at that time was one of the world's oldest domesticated and lucrative industrial crop. This misunderstanding grouped hemp together with marijuana in the Controlled Substances Act making hemp illegal to grow in the USA. This misguided perception was probably perpetuated elsewhere creating lost opportunities of hemp farming in many countries.

If we examine the potential commercial value chain of hemp and related products, it becomes very apparent that this is a lucrative industry. Commercial hemp farming can create global opportunities for South Africa. The size of the global industrial hemp market is poised to reach $10.6 billion by 2025. With all the attention being placed on legalising marijuana, the healthier cousin, hemp and its potential of becoming a mainstream crop in South Africa has been ignored.

Historically hemp was grown industrially for the manufacture of rope, canvas and paper. Today the added usage of hemp has been realised the wellness industry. Hemp seeds are rich in omega-3 and omega-6 fatty acids and has almost as much protein as soybeans. Its richness in vitamin E is beneficial to cardiovascular health. Hemp is also used in clothing fabrics. When combined with cotton or wool, hemp strengthens the fabric resulting in a breathable and comfortable apparel. In a nutshell, hemp can be used in a wide variety of applications and is associated with over twenty-five thousand consumer products. This ranges from hemp apparel and accessories to wellness products and hempseed oil cosmetics.

South Africa is in the middle of a dark economic era. Introducing industrial hemp farming will be a positive move. However, industrial hemp farming in SA is currently not a worthwhile option. The barrier to entry for industrial hemp farming is very high. You still need to get a permit to grow this non-addictive plant. To get this permit, you will need at least 5000 hectors of agricultural land. For South Africa to seriously consider hemp farming, the Department of Agriculture, Forestry and Fisheries (DAFF) must be given the mandate to expand and grow this industry. Unfortunately, hemp like marijuana currently resides with the Department of Health and the Department of Justice. The growth of hemp is regulated in terms of the Medicines and Related Substances Act of 1965 and the Drugs and Drugs Trafficking Act of 1992. Like former President Nixon's misunderstanding, hemp in SA is grouped together with marijuana. Until this legislative red tape is resolved, and hemp is moved to DAFF, industrial hemp farming will not be viable. Now highly, addictive marijuana which is legal for private consumption has an edge over hemp. How does this make any sense at all?

Information and Communication Technology (ICT) Industry – Growth in Tech-Hubs

In a world where the ICT industry and the internet are revolutionising the grounds for competitiveness, knowledge and innovation are essential to economic growth and development. New opportunities have presented itself in developing countries like South Africa, giving rise to a new phenomenon called tech hubs. A tech hub creates a node or incubator for developers, entrepreneurs and investors. Tech hubs tend to focus is on innovation and technology. The main advantage of tech hubs is derived from the notion that companies do not innovate in isolation. Tech hubs provide a cluster of specialised skills, knowledge, and diffusion of ideas creating an environment where knowledge is encouraged to flow through collaborative practices.

Generally, tech hubs are private sector initiatives of ICT communities. They create viable cost effective global economic collaboration previously enjoyed exclusively by large multinational corporations and Governments. This new landscape has made it possible to tap into global possibilities with tech hubs acting as catalysts for small businesses to participate in the global economy. The result is added value to both business and development within the country's economy. A good example of a tech hub is the iHub in Kenya which came into existence in 2010. The purpose of this tech hub was to create a unique space for the Kenyan technological community. It has since become the origin of more than 150 start-up companies and plays host to many technology and innovation related events. The iHub has also many prominent corporate partnerships such as Intel, Microsoft, Google, Nokia, Samsung and Safaricom.

Similarly, South Africa has currently around 59 tech hubs. These create growth in the technology and innovation fields and contribute to service and knowledge-based industries. The pertinent question is whether South Africa is doing enough to take advantage of this new industry? Before I answer this question, let's compare the technology revolution in our country with a less populous country such as Israel. South Africa has a population of 57 million and Israel has a population of 8.9 million. The tech hubs in Israel have given rise to about four thousand start-ups which is more than any other country apart from the USA. Takadu, a hi-tech company formed in a tech hub in 2008 is a good success story. It offers remote smart water global infrastructure monitoring that detect pipe leakages in real-time. One of Takadu's biggest customer is Britain's Thames Water. When a water pipe in London leaks, it will first be picked up by a computer in Israel. It is estimated that the monetary value of Israel's high-tech exports is around $18.4bn a year. The Israeli Government played a key role in this rapid rise by jump starting its high-tech industry. The answer to my earlier question is South Africa is not even close to realising these monetary gains in this industry. So, what's stopping South Africa from capitalising on this new industry? The answer I believe is digital migration.

The International Telecommunications Union held a World Radio Communication conference in 2006 where it was agreed that all countries in Europe, Africa, Middle East and the Iran migrate from analogue to digital broadcasting services by 17 June 2015. South Africa was one of the member states and signatory at the conference. South Africa needed to migrate from analogue to digital broadcasting to free up the spectrum for mobile broadband and other ICT related purposes. Why is this anecdote so important and what does this have to do with the growth of tech hubs?

This migration is vital in unlocking enormous amounts of value in the broadcasting spectrum. Think of the spectrum as being a highway for wireless signals with a fixed number of frequencies or lanes. Analogue signals are currently being used to broadcast free to air television channels like the SABC. These analogue signals can be described with the analogy of slow abnormal vehicles carrying heavy construction machinery driving on the fast lane in the highway. They are very noisy, slow and inefficient preventing other vehicles from using this fast lane. Digital signals are like modern quiet and energy efficient cars that can travel faster and quicker in the fast lane currently being monopolised by the abnormal vehicles. This situation is sabotaging our access to cost-effective and high-speed broadband with a wider coverage. Unfortunately, the original television companies have got the best frequencies for themselves and are broadcasting in analogue format. These frequencies if converted to digital can bring broadband to the poorest rural schools and villages and have our cities buzzing with data moving ten times as fast as the current speed.

On 17 June 2015, South Africa missed the vital deadline of migrating from analogue to digital broadcasting because of its lack of proper planning and implementation. In my opinion this very important project lacked political will. While our politicians and major industry players continue to quarrel over turf and tenders, the opportunity cost of moving to digital broadcasting is increasing exponentially. This means that freeing up our highway-in-the-sky and becoming a major high-tech export player like Israel will remain a pipe dream at least for now.

Information Technology is an industry that South Africa cannot afford to ignore, and digital migration should be a key deliverable in the Ramaphosa Government.

After all it is the platform for the private sector to create more tech hubs that will create more start-ups and ultimately more jobs.

The Drone Industry

The use of unmanned aerial vehicles (UAVs) or drones have burst onto the consumer and business platforms, bringing this sci-fi type technology to reality. Drones are used in many industries for a variety of essential purposes from crop inventory, monitoring in agriculture to eye-in-the-sky coverage in the media industry. This industry has a global monetary value of around $127 billion. The construction industry in Europe is already using drones for aerial surveying in large projects and it has become an essential tool in this industry. This industry is still in its infancy with enormous potential growth capabilities. So why has South Africa not taken advantage of this industry?

The commercial drone legislation in South Africa is onerous and is regulated through the aviation laws equating it to obtaining a license to operate a commercial aircraft. The South African Civil Aviation Authority (SACAA) classifies any commercial drone as an aircraft which must abide by the same laws as a manned aircraft. Just like a commercial pilot, a commercial drone pilot must also go through a similar certification and exams. This can set you back in the region of two hundred thousand rand making the barriers to entry very high. Even with a commercial drone operator's license, operating a drone is subject to unnecessary stringent health and safety regulations discouraging potential investors.

Yet again red tape and onerous legislation is killing a potential industry and South Africa needs to wake up and amend these legislations to grow this industry which will also create new jobs.

Is South Africa's bureaucratic red tape restricting economic growth?

South Africa features unfavourably when one considers the regulatory and bureaucratic burdens of doing business in a country. The highly regulated environment is partially responsible for the mediocre economic performance and contribution of the small business sector. This bureaucracy unnecessarily hampers the development of many business ventures and potential growth.

There is no dispute that South Africa needs to be regulated but not to the extent that it becomes an unacceptable stumbling block preventing economic growth and development. Government has a preference to address the problems it encounters through more regulations. This knee jerk reaction results in more and more red tape without a sound basis for many of these regulations. A good example is the so-called draft policy namely "The Roads Policy." This policy aims to reduce road traffic by introducing a congestion tax. The road infrastructure in South Africa is rapidly deteriorating due to the lack of maintenance caused by blatant corruption, misappropriation of funds and poor planning. Instead of addressing the misuse of funds, Government's response to this problem is to look for other revenue streams over and above the existing levies to plug this shortfall. This congestion tax to private vehicle users is justified under the guise of reducing traffic congestion especially in urban areas. This tax would only make sense if there is a proper, fully functional and safe public transport system. In the current environment, the Government should first address the issue of poor planning and corruption, invest in a good and safe public transport system and only then introduce congestion tax.

Government should be looking at introducing legislation to assist and facilitate processes and not hamper it. They need to ensure that legislations remain relevant and effective over time and should be reviewed periodically. The "Prohibition of the Exhibition of Films on Sundays and Public Holidays Act" for example is a legislation passed in the apartheid era prohibiting people from watching movies on Sunday and public holidays. This Act still exists to this day even though it has lost its relevance. It is imperative that South Africa ditches the unnecessary red tape that is halting any progress within its borders or attracting international investors.

These are only a few illustrations of growing our current industries and entering new industries. These tweaks and fixes can have a positive effect if the will of Government and people are there. We need to think creatively on how we can unburden our current unemployment and economic crisis. Cyril Ramaphosa has been going around the world with his begging bowl looking for foreign investment and trying to sell our country as a good investment despite its domestic problems. Any secured investment is likely to come at a price that ultimately benefits the investor and not South Africa. Instead we should first focus on fixing our country and then attract foreign investors. It reminds me of a quote from the movie "Field of Dreams" which is *"If you build it, he will come."* I will amend this quote to say, *"If we fix our beautiful country, foreign investors will come but this time it will be on our terms"*.

CHAPTER 7: IS CAPITALISM CHOKING DEMOCRACY?

A LTHOUGH SOUTH AFRICA IS A DEMOCRATIC COUNTRY it subscribes to the principles of Capitalism. Capitalism as we know has no limits to the accumulation of wealth. It is based on profit, selfishness and greed, thriving in a highly competitive environment. Considering that nearly half the world's population is living in poverty and suffering immensely, we can surmise that capitalism works for some people but not for all. There is an increasing disparity between Democracy and Capitalism. South Africa is a microcosm of the world's Capitalism landscape and has been an incubator for both Government and Private Sector corruption. We all know that Communism is not a viable alternative to Capitalism. Is there another alternative that is a happy medium between the polar extremes of Capitalism and Socialism?

As a democratic country, we need to ask ourselves a key question - Who is truly in charge of our political economy? Is it the democratically elected government? Are financial institutions or rating agencies in charge? Could it be that a select group of high net worth individuals or large corporations are bankrolling the Ruling Party and other Political Parties? The reality is that citizen participation which is a core element of Democracy, is traded for the interests of the select few individuals and corporations. The obvious result is an oppressive type leadership such as the Zuma Government. There is a distinct gap between participation in a democratic political process and the expected beneficial expectations to the voters. Does the power really lie with the people? Can true democracy exist side by side with capitalism? Let's take a closer look.

On the surface, there is no persuasive argument to assume that Capitalism and Democracy are inseparable. There are instances such as the Chinese economy where Capitalism flourished under autocratic conditions. There are also instances like the current Trump presidency in the USA where Democracy is thriving under autocratic conditions. Even though Capitalism and Democracy evolved around the same time, they have different origins and different fundamental principles. Capitalism as we know it, emerged in England as the result of the Industrial Revolution, while Democracy originated in France being the outcome of the French Revolution. There are deep tensions between these two ideologies. Democracy is contingent on solidarity, whereas capitalists do not care about the people. Democracy is country specific and Capitalism is fundamentally universal and boundaryless. Democracy is built on the equality of the people whereas Capitalism is not concerned with the equitable distribution of wealth. Democracy gives a voice to all its people. In Capitalism the wealthy have by far the loudest voice and this is the one that counts. Despite these differences, history represents these two ideologies as going hand in hand. Two different revolutions, two different ideologies so why is Capitalism driving democratic processes?

Democracies are supposed to give birth to free societies. Instead, capitalism within democratic countries has created a steroidal global economy which is eroding the power of the democratic citizens. The capitalistic bottom line trumps the shared goals of the citizens while Government plays second fiddle to large corporations. On the surface, it appears to be a celestial match. Democracy and Capitalism are publicised as the yin and yang of ideological structures that collectively bring unparalleled global prosperity and freedom to all. In recent years, this pair has shared a common growth platform, where Capitalism has by far been triumphant. Most countries are nowadays part of an integrated and large global market. In the last thirty years, Democracy has experienced a similar accent going from one third of the world's countries having democratic elections to the current two thirds of countries supporting democratic processes.

A common assumption is that where either Capitalism or Democracy thrives, the other is close by supporting its growth. The reality is that their prosperities are beginning to deviate to an extent where Capitalism is thriving, and Democracy is waning into a figurehead. Many economically successful nations like Russia are democracies in name only and have succumbed to the same capitalistic intoxication. This intoxication that is choking the democracies around the world. Corporations and rich individuals control these economies that service their own needs and, in the process, undermine Government's duty to respond to its citizens' needs. True democracy represents free and fair elections promoting a collective vision that brings citizens together to realise a common goal.

The reality is that capitalism within a democratic structure has brought unparalleled prosperity to many but has also widened the inequalities of income and wealth between the haves and have's nots. There is a surge in job insecurity and environmental threats such as global warming. Ideally Democracy should give its citizens the freedom to address the perils of Capitalism in a constructive way. The political powerlessness of the so-called empowered citizens is sabotaging the will of democratic countries to effectively cope with the negative side effects of capitalism.

It is not Capitalism that has failed us. Our selfish greed has distorted the responsibilities of these two ideologies to the detriment of Democracy. The role of Capitalism is to increase the economy and it has succeeded. Democracy on the other hand has struggled to accomplish its own social goal to help citizens collectively achieve both growth and equity. What is desperately needed is for citizens is to stop the capitalistic entities from defining the rules by which they live and become more involved in the political arena. Citizens in democratic countries can alter the rules of the game for the benefit of all. It is so easy for the citizens to relinquish their responsibilities to the large corporations who pretend to possess good corporate citizenship and a moral code of ethics. The reality is that corporations have no personal obligation to resolve social inequalities or save the environment. Their mission is to protect their own bottom line.

Democracy has been largely weakened because corporations are investing heavily in politics, self-promotion and are supporting bribery and corruption. Corporations position themselves to create laws that give them a competitive advantage over their competitors. Their move to influence the political arena is killing the voices of the citizens. Democracy is meant to accomplish a shared pie of economic wealth for all, but its efforts are hampered when corporations use political influence to advance their organisational growth. This is encouraged when greedy Political leaders like Zuma are eager to sacrifice the democratic principles of their party to advance their personal interest. The hypocrisy of trading democratic principles for bigoted loyalty has become a global failure of democratic structures. It is hardly a surprise given the last ten years that South Africa is in this situation. The problem is that most voters especially in the rural areas are blissfully unaware of the reality that they are supporting Political Parties that have been violating their own democratic values and rights.

What is needed is a new mindset built around a holistic concept of a regenerative and democratic economy. While many associate holistic interventions with spiritualists and homeopathic lifestyles, holism focuses on creating a balanced approach to address contradictory issues like collaboration and competition and unity and diversity. Holism supports diversity. It recognises that each nation consists of different people with their own unique traditions and beliefs informed by culture, geographic region and evolving human needs. I present my recommendation on a potential long-term holistic solution to our political muddle.

CHAPTER 8: IS A DIFFERENT AND HONEST POLITICAL APPROACH REALISTIC?

I F WE ARE LOOKING FOR CHANGE we need to do things differently. Equally important is not what we do differently but the mechanisms we put in place to realise a future that we desire. I submit that even if we have the will to create a change, we might still get the future wrong unless we create a framework to implement these change mechanisms that support our vision of the future. Having foresight is virtually the most important aspect of how we see the future. If we can figure our real vision, we can use it to leverage and enable a possible future.

It is therefore imperative to start conceptualising the future. Our future is currently a clean canvas. We can use it to paint our vision to influence the change we want. We need to start thinking about what our new narrative is. For me it is an honest political landscape that works for the people it serves. My father's old narrative of politicians being dishonest must surely be outdated. Is my new and more relevant future of an honest politician realistic?

Is honesty in politics possible?

Is there such a thing as an honest politician? This question goes to the core of democracy. When voters go to the polling booth, they have the expectation that the Political Party that they put their mark against will have their best interest at heart.

However, when politicians turn out to be self-serving and dishonest, citizens just write them off, complain and move on without even voicing their disappointment. This environment becomes a breeding ground for anti-democratic movements to thrive, removing moral values of decency and righteousness from the political arena.

Dishonest politicians are gamblers that put the lives of their voters at risk. They are ruthless and lack humility. These troublemakers pursue their personal greedy ambitions with whatever it takes, irrespective of the risks and the cost to the voters. They are fanatical, dishonest and blinded by the egotistical belief that they are always right. Dishonest politicians are always eager to expose other political parties and publicise a problem in a melodramatic manner. They however lack the willingness to propose feasible solutions.

Fortunately, amidst this ocean of political dishonesty, there are a few honest people like Nelson Mandela. The moral politician wants to chisel out morality within the constraints of a political environment that mimics a distrustful game. The honest politician views politics as a means of achieving a common good for the people. He or she is not naive and understands that compromise, persistence and a strategy of small steps while not losing sight of the objectives, are what is needed to succeed. An honest politician is a person of realistic principles and has the courage to say unpleasant but righteous things. The harshest test that an honest politician faces is when they must defend unpopular ideals that are right. Not everyone succeeds, especially when elections are imminent. Cyril Ramaphosa is a textbook example of a rare honest politician trying to do the right thing in the face of corruption and the looming elections. Sadly, his political campaign trail is accompanied by people enmeshed in corruption and alleged acts of criminal and sexual harassment. But will he do the right thing after the elections?

We must not lose sight of that fact that an honest politician cannot single-handedly succeed in fighting for the common good of the people. Moral politicians need to support each other irrespective of their political affiliations. It is this collective support that will give them the confidence to rise above their political divisions and make morally resourceful decisions. Political morality is not the sole responsibility of politicians and its success is underpinned by the will and involvement of the people.

The citizens must play a part in encouraging this behaviour. We have the power to demand a society comprising of values depicting tolerance, harmony and collective support for individual rights. We must be vocal in rooting out dishonest politicians. Acceptance of political theft and corruption should not be the normal path for politics. This will only attract dishonest people. Honest people tend to shy away from dishonest politics and look to other career paths to make their contribution. We need to demand a life without unequal education, poverty, unemployment, homelessness, hunger, malnutrition and poor health. It is up to us to ensure a moral environment where political dishonesty will not thrive. This will bring honest people to the fore and into politics. What would a moral, people orientated political landscape look like? I submit that we look to countries like Norway to inform the restructuring of our political and social system. Norway is regarded as one of the happiest countries to live in. What does Norway do differently to make its citizens so happy? Let's take a closer look.

Norway is huge on social support where its citizens live in harmony with each other. It comes down to the people supporting each other with Government providing support initiatives for the needy. Citizens feel secure and crime is at its lowest. People live in communities that they can count on for social support. Government proactively creates social areas for people to interact with each other. Most people earn a decent wage and live in proper, comfortable houses. Job security and good working conditions create a secure and happy environment. Norway also offers a variety of options for the unemployed. They have tailored unemployment insurance and child support to suit individual needs.

Norway has a profound sense of community building and the concept of individualism and standing alone is alien to them. Government's commitment to highly subsidised public health care, primary and tertiary education takes this major burden away from its citizens. Primary health care and education is no more seen as a privilege for the rich thus levelling the playing field for everyone. This country offers a caring, free and generous life to its citizens where political honesty and good governance is a reality.

If South Africa wants to emulate Norway, where should we start? With large Corporations misappropriating democracy, I posit that we move away from large corporations and encourage community driven Cooperatives. I am not saying that we should totally eradicate large Corporations. Instead I suggest that we encourage community Cooperatives and cottage industries especially in the rural areas to act as a catalyst for economic development that supports the macro economic growth.

CHAPTER 9:
COMMUNITY
COOPERATIVES – IS THIS
THE ANTIDOTE FOR
POOR ECONOMIC
GROWTH?

C APITALISM, ALTHOUGH CONSIDERED THE BACKBONE of our global economy, is highly dependent on economic growth and becomes unhinged in a negative growth environment. The current economic crisis in South Africa has brought to the fore the implications of an economy without growth. This puts South Africa in a unique position to explore other ways of attaining social and community upliftment. This paradigm must go beyond the myopic capitalistic focus for economic growth that neglects the negative effects of stagnant growth.

Our economic meltdown is a political one. Government has failed to adequately regulate the irresponsible and corrupt behaviour of its Ministers. It has instead allowed looting of the State's resources to happen with impunity. This situation is further exacerbated by our capitalistic economy's blinkered approach focusing solely on growth to the detriment of social sustainability and wellbeing. The ownership structure of a capitalist economy is based on maximisation of profits for the sole purpose of creating wealth and growing shareholder value. Social and environmental issues are seen as an obligatory constraint to be managed within the context of profit maximisation. This limits the rightful focus on social and environmental development thus reducing the positive impact of democracy.

Cooperatives on the other hand are private sector businesses arising from voluntary agreements or associations. Members of Cooperatives are focused on a shared goal of achieving specific social outcomes. Cooperatives are not driven by monetary incentives. They act as a vehicle for willing communities to achieve common social upliftment goals. Cooperatives understand that the societal objectives are more important than financial success and work towards the upliftment and benefit of their members. It is monetary gain that becomes the constraint that needs to be managed in the context of increasing the social benefit to the members. Co-operatives should not be regarded as the 'silver bullet' to solve the poverty crisis. Rather it offers an alternative non-political structure of governance that is better suited to a stagnant poverty-stricken economy.

Large Corporations are still relevant and there must be a balance between the two structures. We need monetary growth but not to the detriment of sustainable wellbeing and prosperity for all. Cooperatives can be introduced as an alternative strategy for rural economic development with the goal of improving the socioeconomic position of the poor people in the rural areas.

Cooperatives in rural areas

Poor people in rural South Africa are facing an overabundance of survival challenges that hinders their active participation in the country's economic activities. Compared to their relatively affluent urban counterparts, they are politically, economically and technologically marginalised. Rural poverty largely affects the Black majority who are landless and unable to make any substantial progress in changing their livelihoods. Urban people are more wealthy and able to influence government to be more biased towards their needs. With extreme poverty in the rural areas and government policies directed at urban areas, the plight of the poor in rural areas has worsened. The enormous development backlogs in the rural areas with respect to education, health, water, electricity, housing and general infrastructure is a testament to Government's urban prejudice. To address rural poverty, there is a need to transform these areas into participative economies. Could Cooperatives be the answer?

The nature of Cooperatives

A Cooperative is formed when an autonomous group of people voluntarily, collectively and democratically get together to form a social organisation to meet their common social, cultural and economic needs. Globally and strategically Cooperatives are suitable instruments to address the development challenges of economic growth while generating employment and reducing poverty. Cooperatives have the potential to respond to rural communities' social and economic needs and become an active participant of the bigger economy. They encourage development within the community by mobilising these resources into a critical mass while maintaining the spirit of the community.

Unlike Corporations where profits are transferred to the shareholders based upon the percentage of ownership, the value in Cooperatives are allocated to its members based upon their patronage and usage. When cooperatives generate value from effective business initiatives, the monies are given to its members in proportion to their patronage. People who utilise the cooperative own it and are responsible for financing and growing it. The governance of the cooperative remains with the members who are responsible for its long-term success. Cooperatives are democratic in their decision-making processes operating solely in the best interest of its members. It is the members who are responsible for managing the Cooperative and are involved at strategic and operational levels.

How do you start a Cooperative?

The first step in forming a Cooperative is to have a business idea supported by likeminded people. These people will become the subsequent members of that Cooperative. This group will then gather information and legal requirements pertaining to their Cooperative. This includes understanding the principles and values of a Cooperative, the ownership culture and what it means to own a business together. Cooperatives are a unique area in our economy where people participate in a democratic way. There needs to be some skills that go into making this venture a success. Formulating the mission and values of the Cooperative is critical and is often overlooked. It is human nature to want to get right down to business. However, mapping the vision, mission and values at inception will come in handy when dealing with problems down the line. If the group does not take time to think through and agree on their mission and shared values, it will become apparent when they face a problem. They will then quickly realise that their perceptions of the

Cooperative's objectives may differ from each other. This will threaten the future of the Cooperative.

The next part is to identify some resources to help the Cooperative move forward. It is critical at this stage to further explore the industry and refine the business concept. Forming a Cooperative will take time and will require financial and social resources. The people forming the Cooperative will need to put in a lot of effort in forming the Cooperative. It is therefore important for the Cooperative to make a major difference in their life and in the lives of their family, friends and the community.

An exploratory meeting would be a good place for the group to present their concept to others who may be interested. It is at this time a steering committee could be formed. It is important that key people from the industry and the community are included in this committee. These members must understand basic business finance principles and have credibility within the local community. This is also the time to get monetary contributions from interested parties. There will be some incidental costs involved in organising a Cooperative. This contribution is also a good indicator of the commitment and interest of the people.

The next step is conducting a feasibility study, which is basically a broad-brush insight into the industry in question. This analysis will look at the viability of the concept, the market potential, technical aspects, capital requirements and financial projections. Only if the feasibility study confirms the viability of the concept and the steering committee ratifies these findings, should the next process of compiling a business plan proceed.

A business plan is a detailed look at the proposal for this venture. This is where pertinent industry details from the feasibility study is extracted supporting the Cooperative's focus area. A description of the product or the service offering, marketing plan, operational details such as the organisation and management structure and financial plan forms part of the business plan. The board of directors are appointed, and membership equity funding requirements become enforceable. There are various ways to go about funding a Cooperative. This includes an initial equity and an annual membership contribution. The Cooperative may also collect transaction fees. It is common for example in agricultural Cooperatives to have some type of surcharge on each item sold. There may be a percentage surcharge on every product bought through an agricultural Cooperative. Once all this is done and the legal and administration requirements are met, the new Cooperative is open for business.

Creating a Cooperative sounds well and good but how realistic and practical is it? Does it deliver in reducing poverty, creating employment and stimulating the economy? To answer these questions, let's look at a successful Cooperative initiative in Africa. Let's look at Kenya.

Kenya's Cooperative Movement

Kenya has a rich history of Cooperatives in communities especially in the informal sector. After independence from Britain in 1963 there was a strong emphasis on the post-independence development policies. This initiative was referred to as the Harambee spirit which in Swahili means "collectively pulling together". It was critical in achieving post-independence land reclamation from the departing foreigners. Kenyans were motivated to collectively build their own country in accordance to their specific needs. They used the Harambee ideology to raise funds for the many post-independence development projects. It is still used as a process to resolve issues or to undertake developments that cannot be accomplished by a single person alone.

Cooperative developments are found in the educational sector. These developments include construction of rural schools and obtaining capital to fund colleges. On the social front they include orphanages and rural health care centres. Infrastructurally they include the construction of proper rural roads and reservoirs. Other examples of this collectivism include but is not limited to rural citizens assisting each other with the planting, weeding, spraying or even harvesting their crops as opposed to paying someone to do it. An example of positive Cooperatives developments in rural Kenya is a group of citizens in the Migori district of Nyanza province. These citizens started their own soy bean production and processing facilities using the Cooperative model.

Ironically the Harambee ideology in Kenya can be traced back to White Colonists forming cooperative movements with the sole purpose of getting resources at reasonable rates and marketing their agricultural products. These Cooperatives excluded the indigenous Kenyans denying them of similar benefits in forming their own Cooperatives. These agricultural Cooperatives were formed in areas with the best fertile land, like the great Rift Valley Province. They targeted regions that supported growing cash crops such as tea and coffee providing huge income to the Colonialists. Since independence, agricultural Cooperatives have gained popularity especially in the rural areas. In 2008 alone, these Cooperatives created just under two million jobs either directly or indirectly.

Apart from employment, Cooperatives have important roles to play in Kenya. They for example facilitate the processing and marketing of a large percentage of agricultural products such as coffee, cotton and dairy. They initiate saving opportunities from both the formal and the informal sectors and offer loans to budding entrepreneurs. Kenya has a national cooperative college called the Cooperative College of Kenya situated in Nairobi. This is a semi-autonomous government training institution. It was established by the Kenyan Ministry of the Cooperative Development and Marketing with the intention of providing cooperative education and training. It collaborates with similar institutions both nationally and internationally to improve research and education in Cooperatives. Such initiatives bear testament to the importance of Cooperatives in economic growth.

Looking at the differences between Cooperatives and Corporations, we find that Cooperatives are formed to provide goods and services to its members as opposed to making profit from its customers. It is owned and controlled by its members who are directly involved and make use of the services of the Cooperative. The primary objective of a Cooperative is not to make profits but rather to directly satisfy the needs of its members. Unlike a typical Corporation, the control of this democratic system does not lie in the number of shares each member holds. The distinction of a Cooperative is its clearly defined rights of participation using the one-member one-vote system. Members share any surplus according to their patronage and how much business they have done through the Cooperative. In the case of a Corporation, investors with more money own more shares giving them more votes and control and more profits. Members of a Cooperative are also more attentive towards developing the community. In a nutshell Cooperatives are a union of individuals bringing the needs of the Community to the fore. Corporations can be described as a monetary union bringing the needs of the shareholders to the fore.

This optimism about Cooperatives especially in rural areas has the potential to grow the local economy. Nurturing Cooperatives into profitable organisations can contribute positively to the microeconomic enhancement of the rural areas. What is South Africa's stance on Cooperatives?

CHAPTER 10: WHAT IS THE CURRENT STATE OF COOPERATIVES IN SOUTH AFRICA?

L IKE KENYA, SOUTH AFRICA HAS A LONG HISTORY of agricultural Cooperatives. In the early 1900s' many Cooperatives, especially agricultural Cooperatives were formed and like Kenya it excluded Black farmers from participating in agricultural Cooperatives. It was around this time that several Acts were passed that allowed Government to assist farmers. The most pertinent Act was the establishment of the Land Bank in 1912. The purpose of this Act was to legitimise the settlement of White farmers on land owned by Government and in the future agricultural land purchased by the State. White farmers were further assisted by the Cooperative Societies Act established in 1922. The main purpose of this Act was to assist farmers in marketing and selling their supplies which resulted in attractive subsidies in the agricultural sector.

In 1994, our democratic Government tried to address the disparities of White Cooperatives that originated during the apartheid era. Cooperatives formed after 1994 had the support of Government in the form of grants and resources and training with many of these initiatives targeting previously disadvantaged people. The previous White agricultural Cooperatives that dominated the processing, pricing, finance and marketing sectors became obsolete and several of these Cooperatives became investor-orientated organisations.

Sadly, the mortality rate of Cooperatives formed after 1994 is very high. In fact, the Cooperatives Act of 2005 specifically targeted Black people in rural areas yet the level of success of Cooperatives enjoyed in other countries has not been realised in South Africa. Even with the introduction of various financial assistance such as the Cooperative Incentive Scheme, Cooperatives are underperforming. The Cooperative sector continues to consistently underperform despite the increase in Government support. Why is it so difficult for these Cooperatives to survive amidst such sound policies and support?

What's wrong with the sustainability of Cooperatives?

The whole perception of Cooperatives in South Africa is wrong – very wrong. There is a misconception that Cooperatives are mechanisms that geriatric or unemployed people use to get monetary assistance from Government. Furthermore, in the rural areas, Cooperatives are not entirely independent. They are run in an autocratic way where members do not make decisions without consulting with their traditional leaders. Other challenges include the lack of members' commitment causing difficulty in managing and operating the Cooperative. This is further exacerbated by constraints such as a lack of access to finance despite Government funding, lack of resources and infrastructure and in the case of agricultural Cooperatives – lack of access to land.

Non-compliance of financial reporting as required by the Cooperative Act of 2005 has also led to the demise of many Cooperatives. Lack of Cooperative governance threatens the sustainability of Cooperatives. Other contributing factors are inadequate developmental programmes and the lack of members' expertise in managing and marketing their Cooperatives. In a nutshell, the success of Cooperatives has been compromised by their operational structures and lack of skills making it difficult to have a cohesive management vision and assigning operational resource responsibilities to its members.

Are Cooperatives still a viable option?

Putting the negative experiences aside, Cooperatives could still play a significant role in our country's economic growth, employment creation and poverty alleviation. Success factors of Cooperatives are good quality products, appropriate skills and management training. Knowledge of profitable enterprises, good marketing skills, up to date administrative compliances and exploiting technology are also important.

Like Kenya, South Africa should have a proper department for Cooperatives instead of incorporating it under the Department of Trade and Industry. This ministry should have centres especially in rural areas that market and support Cooperatives. The centres should offer courses and guidance on managerial skills and financial matters. These centres will give members practical knowledge to manage Cooperatives in a professional manner while monitoring the success of these ventures. This new ministry must align itself with Government's development goals of reducing poverty and starvation. It must also target goals of providing affordable healthcare, quality education, housing, decent employment, economic growth and reducing inequalities between the rich and poor.

The new department can assist small Cooperatives to transform into profitable and sustainable large Cooperatives by providing technical, business and financial assistance. This transformation will lead to productive enterprises especially in the rural areas thus creating employment. Transforming small Cooperatives into large Cooperatives is critical in creating a country with a broad economic base. South African Cooperatives are crying out for management education and training. In response to this need, this new department should partner with current accredited training service providers and institutions to offer relevant training programmes. Universities need to be encouraged to participate in strategies that expand and extend their academic services to the Cooperative sector. The partnership between Government, training institutions and Cooperative stakeholders will create a democratic process in crafting and implementing sustainable programmes in this sector.

Promoting Cooperatives in various business sectors would be a positive move towards uplifting the social and economic position of the poor and reducing the poverty gap. The new department must act as the mediator between the Cooperatives and other government departments responsible for delivering services to these Cooperatives. This can be achieved by service level agreements between these departments and Cooperatives outlining the obligations of these departments associated with delivering their services to Cooperatives. If these interventions are put in place, we will have a chance at creating sustainable Cooperatives with which to bolster our crippling economy.

Cooperatives are vital mechanisms for poverty alleviation and job creation. They introduce an alternative form of economic and social growth with goals that are social, environmental, and community driven as opposed to been purely capitalistic.

The voices of the marginalised poor and rural groups are strengthened creating a platform for these groups to participate in and benefit from the economy of South Africa. Cooperatives are a positive way to go. Apart from Cooperatives, is there anything that ordinary South Africans can do differently to get our country back on track?

CHAPTER 11: WHAT SHOULD SOUTH AFRICANS BE DOING?

N ATIONAL ELECTION DAY IS AROUND THE CORNER and, as the media coverage predicts, the outcome of this election will be as momentous as the first democratic elections in 1994. I predict that voter turnout will be just as high. The young voters will probably be the most influential if their turnout is high. But will there be a change, and will the change really benefit the people of South Africa?

There is an assumption in our democratic country that voting is our only civic duty. The rest is left to Government to create positive economic growth and a functional Democracy. Sadly, this attitude is too narrow, and we are only paying lip service to Democracy. A truly democratic society demands more than a tick against a political party in a ballot sheet every five years or so. True Democracy is realised by the actions and behaviours we exhibit in our everyday lives. Democracy involves the collective effort of its citizens in running communities and non-profit organisations. It involves healthy debates with each other and finding compromises that we can all live with. Democracy encourages celebrating our differences and finding unity in this diversity. It is only when we are living in this way and supporting these ideals will we have a thriving Democracy.

Citizens in a purely capitalistic society are conflicted. Being part of the global economy, they want affordable consumer goods and high returns on their investments. However, there is a social trade-off that comes with these wants. It is easy to blame Corporations for the social problems that arise. However, the material desires of the Citizens encourage Corporations to trade their employee wellbeing and benefits for profits. Environmental issues also are totally ignored. Corporations sacrifice their social and community loyalties and morph into money machines. Chief Executive Officers and their Executives take home exorbitant salaries. They have no concern in addressing social inequalities or protecting the environment. They robotically focus on protecting the bottom line.

Citizens in truly democratic society are not similarly constrained. Their needs are more Community orientated. They can change policies in favour of Community upliftment. True Democracy accomplishes goals that we cannot achieve as individuals. This Democratic utopia looks good on paper but is it practical? Realistically we cannot totally abolish Capitalism, but we also need a sound Democracy. The good news is that it is possible grow a resilient Democracy in a capitalistic environment. It is possible to have a balance between Capitalism and Democracy, but it requires daily effort and involvement from the citizens.

Voting and social participation in Democracy are related yet interdependent goals. An election offers the obvious singular opportunity that reinforces the collective principles and practices of Democracy. However, these practices should be habitual and omnipresent. As citizens of South Africa, engaging in civic opportunities should become common practice. You do not have to be a politician or a Government official to participate in community upliftment projects. We must strive to become a compassionate, participative nation working and progressing together.

We can first start by understanding and celebrating our diversity instead of looking at each other with stereotypical suspicion. Contrary to the race nonsense our Politicians are shoving down our throats, we all have the same needs and goals. Political campaigns that promote racial divisions are just ruses to delude us into voting for them. South Africa became a democracy in 1994. Instead of fulfilling the dream of a rainbow nation, we are still living in an apartheid divided society. The only visible change is middle class Black people moving into the previously White neighbourhoods. Yes, apartheid was an atrocious act against humanity and took away the dignity of many people. But we need to move forward and stand together if we have any chance of uplifting South Africa.

The Ruling Party has messed up badly and brought South Africa to its knees with its greed and corruption. Luckily our justice system is still sound, but it moves very slowly. The various Commissions are bringing corruption to the fore and I believe that the culprits will eventually be prosecuted. We can choose to sit back and criticise the ANC and lament over our failing economy and lifestyle. This will not change the status quo of our current situation. We can also choose to get together as a nation trusting each other, working together and uplifting each other. We need to collectively be part of the change and actively pull each other out this crippling situation. Collectively we can make South Africa a better place for all. We need each other irrespective of our racial identity.

Should we focus on the Youth?

Getting the Youth to be more socially involved is a good place to start. Generally, secondary and tertiary educational institutions are places that shape their identities. These institutions can be used to encourage the Youth to flex their young civic muscles. They can encourage the Youth to engage in adult like politics but in a controlled environment. These institutions will allow them to explore a wide range of ideas across the political spectrum. They will become incubators for healthy social gatherings and debates. Tertiary institutions especially are democratic microcosms providing a relatively safe setting to embrace different political ideologies. They are facilities for the Youth to develop a healthy conviction of civic duties that will be with them forever. Exposing the Youth to rich yet practical democratic experiences is critical in attaining the individual and social goals of a more sustainable democracy.

The democratic curriculum can form part of the educational experience. Solid democratic initiatives can be implemented in several ways, aligning educational institutions with community needs. These initiatives may include inviting learner participation in mock government scenarios, fostering humanitarian relations and projects, encouraging racial and cultural integration while celebrating diversity. Let's try and unite the Youth through their diversity.

What about Moral Leaders?

For this ideology to be effective, a great emphasis must be placed on moral leadership because only true leaders with Mandela's spirit can take our country forward. A moral leader is one that demonstrates a personal example of honesty, is dedicated to the welfare of everyone, has moral conviction and inspires and guides people towards a promising future. A moral leader is one that will step forward and bring a new progressive era to the people by minimising exploitation and violence and making progress happen as soon as possible. A true leader will put an end to the suffering of the masses.

These leaders exist amongst us but sadly not in the political sphere. They have shunned politics because of its toxic and corrupt persona. Even though the outcome of the coming elections is pivotal to our future democracy, many of us are conflicted about which Political Party to vote for. I believe that I am not alone in feeling that none of our political leaders are truly for the people. These Parties see us as a tick on a ballot sheet that can potentially get them as many seats in Parliament as possible. If I look at the bickering between the Parties in Parliament, it is obvious that our needs are forgotten. The political aspirations of the Party are their top priority. I personally cannot see any of them striving for true Democracy.

We need a Political Party with leaders that will challenge the dishonest status quo that has dogged politics throughout history. We need honest leaders to get into politics and clean up the mess once and for all. I challenge leaders like Professor Thuli Madonsela to leave the comfort of Academia and get into politics. My message to Sipho Pityana, Makhosi Khoza and Bonang Mohale is to leave their current vocation and move into politics. South Africa needs honest leaders like them. Their reputation precedes them and if they form a Political Party, I will vote for them as I will be voting for true Democracy. I will be voting for change. A personal note to Makhosi Khoza – I would have voted for her new Political Party and was so disappointed when she canned it.

We need to understand that true Democracy requires our committed effort to grow our country economically and socially fostering a diverse nation that is proud to be South African. Ideally the role of Government should be more supportive. Government should be providing the sound infrastructural backbone to support our efforts in moving South Africa forward. Sitting back and doing nothing and leaving everything to Government is not true Democracy.

On Wednesday, 8 May 2019, I hope that everyone including our youth will turn out in record numbers to vote for whichever Political Party that inspires them. Collectively we have a strong voice and are politically empowered to move our country forward. The real work will happen after the elections with everyone being actively involved. This effort will hopefully foster an environment of compassion for each other and aspirations for a truly robust Democracy. Remember, we all belong to this country that is our South Africa.

CONCLUDING
THOUGHTS

THE SOLUTIONS I PUT FORWARD reflect my opinion of what should be done. They are by no means a total solution to our problems. They represent a snapshot of my ideas for solving our crisis. My dream is to galvanise South Africans to actively and peacefully find a platform to bring their own ideas and solutions to the fore. I have emerged from my comfort zone by writing this book on politics. Sharing our own unique suggestions will create opportunities to bring our country back to its full glory. I am sure that ordinary citizens like myself have amazing and realistic solutions in their minds and all we need is an outlet to share them. So, create a blog or perhaps form an Educational Cooperative in a rural area. Just get your solutions and ideas out there. Together we can make that difference and move our country forward.

Getting justice for the corrupt culprits of state capture will take a very long time. It is hard to believe that the ANC that gave our country freedom and Democracy is the same organisation that has caused so much destruction taking away the hope of so many citizens. With Zuma at the helm, the ANC virtually cannibalised itself and its ideology. We can complain about the current mess that we are in, cursing the ANC for destroying our future and the future of our children. The privileged few can sit back and lament on their so-called good apartheid days. We can choose to look at each other with suspicion and blame each other for our dire situation. Maybe this will temporary soothe our sad situation, but it will not change anything.

Perhaps we can take a different approach by taking control of our lives and needs. Instead of putting our dreams in the hands of our Politicians in the hope that they will fulfil them, take control of the future. Get involved and collectively navigate our country towards our future in the direction we see fit. We can do it. Together we have the voice that will be heard even amidst the political corruption and horse trading.

I am sure that your first response to my suggestion is that this is just another ludicrous pipedream. I remember when I was in primary school we had a subject called Creative Writing. This was one of my favourite subjects because we could write about whatever was on our mind. It so happened that at one Creative Writing session my mind was blank, and I could not think of anything to write about. In desperation I wrote about a joke a friend had told me the previous day and submitted it. My teacher found it hilarious and was in stitches with laughter. I received high marks for this submission. After that session the rest of my classmates followed suit and submitted their jokes as well. This changed our future Creative Writing sessions. Not only was this subject creative, it was also full of fun and laughter. The purpose of this anecdote is to illustrate that a small change is all we need to refocus our energy into redefining our purpose in this Democracy. We can make the change if we develop the will to do so. Hopefully this book is just the catalyst we need.

The following Mandela quote is an inspiration to start afresh:
"Let there be justice for all. Let there be peace for all. Let there be work, bread, water and salt for all. Let each know that for each, the body, the mind and the soul have been freed to fulfil themselves." **Nelson Mandela (Inaugural Speech, 10 May 1994)**
Together we can do it. Let's strive for real Democracy.

Let South Africa shine the beacon of honest politics to the world. Let South Africa strive for honest, non-corrupt political leadership that serves its people and not the needs of the Political Party or their funders. Let the people of South Africa show the world that they can run a truly democratic country thriving with unity and honest politics. Let South Africa show the world that there is more to gain from serving the ordinary people as opposed to servicing the pockets of corrupt Politicians and their allies. Let South Africa demonstrate that even amidst such political corruption, poverty, anarchy and turmoil, the will of ordinary honest citizens can turn this country around. Let South Africa shine.

www.ingramcontent.com/pod-product-compliance
Lightning Source LLC
Chambersburg PA
CBHW051401280526
45784CB00007B/3045